SPIRITUALITY AND INDIAN CULTURE

By the Same Author

Freedom of the Soul: A Post-Modern Understanding of Hinduism

About the Author

Dr. M.M. Agrawal read western philosophy at University of London and subsequently taught it at various Universities abroad. In India, he has been a fellow at the Indian Institute of Advanced Study, Shimla. Also, he held the Chair of Culture at North-Eastern Hill University, Shillong.

Agrawal has many books to his credit, including *Individuality and Reincarnation* (1978), *The Philosophy of Non-attachment* (1982), *Consciousness and the Integrated Being* (1991), *Ethics and Spirituality* (1998), and *Freedom of the Soul* (2003).

SPIRITUALITY AND INDIAN CULTURE

M.M. Agrawal

CONCEPT PUBLISHING COMPANY, NEW DELHI-110059

Cataloging in Publication Data—DK
Courtesy: D.K. Agencies (P) Ltd. <docinfo@dkagencies.com>

Agrawal, M. M. (Murari Mohan), 1937-
Spirituality and Indian culture / M.M. Agrawal.
p. cm.
Includes bibliographical references.
Includes index.
ISBN 8180692329

1. Spiritual life—Hinduism. 2. India—Civilization—Philosophy.
I. Title.

DDC 297.544 21

ISBN-81-8069-232-9

First Published 2005

Published and Printed by
Ashok Kumar Mittal
Concept Publishing Company
A/15-16, Commercial Block, Mohan Garden
NEW DELHI-110059 (India)

Phones : 25351460, 25351794
Fax : +91-11-25357103
Email : publishing@conceptpub.com

PREFACE

This book has emerged from my reflections in Philosophy of Culture which I taught for several years at North East Hill University in Shillong. Since this course was in the department of Philosophy, it had to have a philosophical edge rather than an anthropological or literary. It was not a very difficult goal to achieve as soon as I realized that Indian culture is so heavily indebted to, and indeed rooted in, the Indian philosophical traditions. But since the philosophical traditions are themselves rooted in the most ancient spiritual and religious traditions, the culture of India must be understood by reference to the sacred and the extraordinary quest of Truth which the Indian intellect and imagination so passionately engaged in.

This most incredible culture of India is rightly assessed as the best example of a sustained evolutionary exercise in "enquiry" which the human mind has conducted in ancient times. The philosophical insights concerning the nature of Existence, which appeared as spiritual realizations to the seekers of Truth, seeped into the entire web of human communities living in India and shaped their ways of life most profoundly. All along and everywhere the most central realizations were never forgotten. Most importantly the view of reality alluded to in the ancient scripture of Rig Veda, where it is described as "one divine reality" from which all existence emanates, has provided an extraordinary sense of the unity of life, its integrity and its meaningful evolutionary goals. Thus the Indian culture came upon the exhaltation and celebration of dictums like "Vasudhaiva Kutumbkam" meaning 'the world is one family', and "Ekam Satya Vipra Bahudha Vadanti" meaning 'truth is one but the learned express it differently'. This background of fundamental insight into the nature of reality is what explains the extraordinary variety and the 'unity in diversity' of Indian culture. This is also what explains the central value of an unending quest of Truth, Goodness and Beauty which informs all cultural endeavours in India and yields the framework of virtues of tolerance, non-violence and compassion which constantly engage our minds and guide in shaping our social, intellectual, artistic and political institutions.

If my intuition about this holy alliance between Indian spirituality and its culture is correct, then, surely, this study opens up a new approach to any serious attempt in understanding Indian culture.

New Delhi **M.M. Agrawal**

ACKNOWLEDGEMENTS

I am grateful to Professor K.C. Baral and Professor S.C. Malik for incisive discussions and enlightement on the issues covered in this book, and to Miss Ann Patcharin for help in preparing the manuscript.

M.M. Agrawal

CONTENTS

1

INTRODUCTION

Cultural in its most general definition is the way of life of a people. The people concerned are identified as one entity by their geographical location and history. When the Persian King Cyrus the Great, living in the sixth century BC, coined the word HINDU to describe the people who lived around and beyond the Indus, he was using both these criteria, since the Indus river roughly marked the eastern boundary of his kingdom.

And how is a way of life identified? Firstly, it is the major forms of activities, recurring and relatively permanent, which the people concerned engage in their communal life. But human action cannot be understood simply in terms of their gross manifestations in behaviour. Behind their activities lies a gamut of values, vision and insight concerning the nature of reality, which constitute their attitudes, motives and intentions in life.

It is this 'software', as it were, that makes their activities intelligible in human terms. Next, the way of life is manifest in the forms of life they create in their relationships. These refer to the way they relate to each other in family and friendship, in religion and business, at work and leisure, in art and entertainment and so on, and also how they relate to nature in general and to material objects of civilization.

However, in the modern world an extraordinary thing has taken place. The 'structures' that embody these activities and relationships, both in the material world such as farming, and in the social world such as in marriage, are rapidly changing. The impact of modern science and technology is so strong and dynamic that all forms of existing structures soon become unrecognizable and even disappear from social life. New forms of life are constantly emerging and keeping the human society in constant flux. Now, in such a situation the criterion of identity of a culture shifts to the level of the software I have spoken of.

Primarily it is the values, insights and attitudes that give meaning to life in a community. A culture is a map of the meaning of life of a community. In the case of India, this software is most comprehensively stored up in Hinduism. The roots of modern Hinduism are to be found in the ancient religious/philosophical scriptures of the Vedas. From the earliest days of the *Rig Veda* (believed to have been composed around 3000 BC), its faith and spirituality has been evolving and assimilating new ideas. Yet what is amazing is that the Rig Vedic central vision of reality was never abandoned.

In the *Rig Veda* the enquirer refers to the knowledge "that I am the universe" but admits in humility, not knowing it experientially. He says that "due to bondage to actions based in the knowledge of the outward-oriented mind", he is ignorant of this unity with the whole (*RV* 1, 164, 37). In the past, culture and religion coalesce in the unified concept of *Dharma*. In this concept, culture is seen as the quest of human perfections which falls in three primaeval cognizances, epistemic, moral and aesthetic respectively. Culture is the quest of Truth, Goodness and Beauty; corresponding to these cognizances. Culture grows by absorbing knowledge and thus, one can see why there should be cultural diversity. However, cultures can be compared in terms of their relative absorption of knowledge, internal consistency and the overall coverage of the width of life. Since life is an open-ended affair and truth, goodness and beauty are inexhaustible in themselves, a closed culture will be inferior to an open one.

Indian culture values freedom in a holisitic perception most and therefore, retains its openness. Freedom is a necessity to further the human quest of perfections and also, ontologically, an end in itself. Indeed, in its spiritual accretions, freedom is the ultimate end of life and includes in its consciousness, the Hindu trinity of truth, goodness and beauty in their highest manifestations. Its consciousness is best described by Shankara as "*sat, chit* and *anand*", which refers to the three basic formal aspects of reality, namely truth, consciousness and bliss. This idea of freedom was later to become the pivotal notion of a large number of spiritual endeavours of Indian people to understand reality philosophically and to access it in its normally hidden form, in religious practices. It is this variety of extraordinary insights and practices which have been evolving in interaction with each other which are now available under one title of "Hinduism".

For thousands of years, Hindu insights, values and motivations have shaped the Indian culture in its search of human perfections in the Arts, Sciences and Literature so profusely that today in spite of the presence of religions of non-Indian origin in India, we can safely say that Indian culture is predominantly Hindu.

The influence of Indian spirituality over Indian culture is a widely acknowledged fact of history. This spirituality is a common nexus to all the religions of Indian origin and through mysticism, it has been significantly assimilated in other religions which flourish on the Indian soil. It is interesting to note that Christianity was not originally brought to India by any Church. It was introduced by the apostle St. Thomas himself which 100 Brahmin families of Kerala embraced. These Brahmins were already mentally prepared for a new incarnation by their own Hindu beliefs, which prophecied one for our own age of *Kalyuga*. This common spirituality is available to mankind through the earliest Hindu scripture called the *Rig Veda*. The Vedic spirituality, later developed philosophically in the meditations of the *Upanishadas,* is contained most comprehensively in what is known today under the title "Hinduism". Thus, the spirit of enquiry, the humility of admitting ignorance, the freedom of discussion, and the quest of the experience of the eternal, introduced in the beginning of *Rig Veda*, remain the hallmark of Indian spirituality until today. It sees the Universe as "One Divine Reality" (*Rig Veda* 10, 129, 3) called *Brahman* and speaks of it as the source from which everything emanates, including the gods, the whole of nature, all the worlds, and even the Supreme Being, considered as the personal God called *Ishwara* (*Rig Veda* 1,164, 46).

In this vision the *Purusha,* i.e. the aspect of pure universal conscious intelligence, enters into *Prakriti* (the dormant essence of material reality) and the union of the two creates life and the living earth as we know it. Thus, the whole so-called creation is the result of the embodiment of *Purusha*, this is the explanation of why the Hindus regard all the forces of nature and their large embodiments, such as rivers, mountains, forests and seas as sacred and worship them accordingly. This gives a sense of reverence of nature as a whole. It is only the colonial intellectuals (who must have known this philosophy of nature) who deliberately ignore the sacredness of nature. They treat the worship of rivers etc. as an *ad hoc* phenomenon, so that they can equate it with superstition. In the *Gita*, also Krishna, speaking as the incarnate God says:

> The Earth, Water, Fire and Air
> Space, the Mind, the Intellect
> And the Ego, are all
> My eight-fold distinct natures.[1]

In ancient India, *Dharma* signified the framework values for a way of life. It did not mean religion proper as it is understood today. It meant a way of life, a culture, regulated within a framework of those values which are seen to be conducive to the overall spiritual end of life. It is a teleological conception which is sensitive to characteristically human dimensions of existence. It considers man as a whole—biological, mental and spiritual—and maintains that living one's life according to the order and discipline of *Dharma* brings about the, holistic development and flourishing of the human being. In this perspective, *Dharma* is the same as the proper meaning of culture.

Of course, there is a lot of confusion about the proper meaning of culture, because in the modern western studies, it was originally introduced by the anthropologists who studied only the operative beliefs and the traditions of tribal communities. But today culture has taken the central stage in social studies generally. The word '*sanskriti*' in Sanskrit language, meaning 'culture' has acquired its usage only in recent times. Hinduism has assimilated several thousand years of spiritual and religious experiences, insights and attitudes of seers, saints and philosophers of many different persuasions. Yet it has maintained its connectivity with the Vedas. It has gone through various stages of religious knowledge, and through its famous epics of *Mahabharata* and *Ramayana* and a multitude of other religious literatures and made them available to the general public. Amazingly, it is also available to the illiterate masses through the strong oral traditions of communitarian recitations of religious texts and through performative arts especially singing of devotional songs by wandering monks and mystics. Religious thoughts and emotions seep into most of our daily activities. Indian culture is predominantly religious. Though secularism has been embraced in politics, in culture it is still a long way away from it. Religion in the form of Hinduism has shown an extraordinary sense of adoption and adaptation. Its unity in multiplicity of religious strands, its Vedic faith in *vasudhev kutumbkum* (mankind is one family), its feeling of sacredness for human potential of creativity, its passion for deep freedom of the soul and love of nature is what makes it the most popular religion of such a diversity of ethnic communities as we find in India.

The *Rig Vedic* gnomic apothem of "One Divine Reality" is the single most important guiding concept for the subsequent unity of Hinduism. Though Hinduism is frequently polytheistic and often atheistic (as in the philosophies of *Samkhya Yoga*), the Vedic vision of Reality did eventually provide a robust monotheism (implied in the *Rig Veda* 1, 164, 20, where the divine is referred to as *Paramatma* or the supreme soul, and distinguished from *Jivatma* or the individual soul) or the belief in One Personal God, the Supreme Being called *Ishwara*, without the loss of its polytheistic or non-theistic background. This is most characteristic of Hinduism—a remarkable synthesis of the One and the Many. In it we have the concept of a One called *Brahman* which is considered as the transcendent source of the Many. The Many including the various gods of the Vedas that emanate from the One which is represented as eternal, without a beginning or end, remaining undiminished and unchanged in the course of emanation. And this idea is linked to the mystical conceptions in the *Upanishadas* of *Moksha* through self-knowledge, or the final liberation, in which the individual soul returns to the ultimate source of *Brahman*. This strand of a mystical union of the individual with the divine is shared not only by all the religions of Indian origin but others as well that flourish in the country.

This idea of ascent or return of the soul to *Brahman*, later formulated in the famous *Advaita* or Non-Dualistic philosophy of Shankaracharya, is a rich source of Indian mysticism, both in its non-theistic as well as theistic renditions. In its theistic version it represents the *Bhakti Marg*, the path of love and devotion of God, in which the seeker of God reunites with the divine source. This marriage of religion and philosophy should not surprise anyone, because in India philosophy was always considered as an experiential path (therefore named *Darshana*) to religious knowledge of the eternal truth. Intellectual perception is not separated from higher spiritual intuitions. It is a holistic movement of consciousness. The perception of truth is united with Love of the divine in a mystical experience of the One. The *Bhakti Marg*, as distinguished from *Gyan Marg* or the path of knowledge, is what is culturally more significant at the ground level. But the distinction between the two paths eventually disappears at the spiritual level where *bhakti* culminates into *gyan*. As the *Gita* assures:

> Those who came to me in surrender
> Desiring freedom from rebirth
> I gave them surely, the complete
> Knowledge of Brahman and spiritual action.[2]

The *bhakti* movement took firm roots since the writing of the *Mahabharata* in which Krishna as the incarnation of Vishnu plays out a full human drama from the childhood to his final disappearance from the human world. With the doctrine of incarnation, first propounded in Hindu scriptures, mankind finds a completely new perspective upon the knowledge of the divine. Since the incarnate God lives on the earth and plays out a human life experiencing and transforming his emotions in this process, man is able to communicate directly with the divine and learn of the truth in a way in which he could not do if he had no reference to the immanence of divinity in the human life. In the *Gita*, Krishna teaches:

> As and when *Dharma* declines and Evil abounds, I incarnate to protect the righteous and reestablish the order of Good.[3]

In one stroke he has freed the human mind from his anxieties over the unknown and his own potential in relation to it. Man knows that he is not sharply separated from the divine and his return or unity with the divine is a real possibility for him.

Theistic Hinduism was originally polytheistic. In the *Rig Veda*, the earliest document on personal gods, several divinities are mentioned, and hymns written in their praise were embodied in prayers used in the myriad practices of worship. The worship of these gods was usually accomplished by what is called *Havana* i.e., a sacrificial sacrament in which offerings are placed in a small burning pyre while chanting mantras (sacred invocations) in praise of the particular divinity being worshipped. The fire which is itself a divinity is believed to be the carrier of the sacrifices to the god worshipped. *Rig Veda* records Varun as the most powerful of the gods.

Each god has a major kind of power associated with his personality and manifest in the universe, who is represented as the embodiment of a network of natural attributes with the centrality of the major power. The divinities were imagined in their embodiments resembling human-like forms. This is only logical. Since a personal god listens to your prayers and shows qualities of charity, courage, piety and justice it is only natural to imagine him embodied like humans. The logic here is that just as a smile without a face is unintelligible so the manifestation of psychological attributes without appropriate bodily expressions and behaviour is unintelligible.

However, at all times their connection with Brahman is not forgotten. As we have said, Brahman is the source of all energy. This source is the divine Reality. It is infinite in all conceivable ways. The gods emanate from this reality which is spiritual and transcendent to our knowledge of cosmic reality. Gods are the parts of the manifest cosmos. And anything that manifests in the cosmos as an individual entity can have only a limited number of attributes. There cannot be, logically, any manifestation of all the infinitely infinite number of attributes which the unmanifest Brahman possesses. So it makes sense, given the conception of "One Divine Reality" which is infinite in all conceivable ways, to imagine a number of gods each of limited number of attributes, appearing spontaneously in the self-organising universe.

The idea of one supreme being as the personal god was also natural to emerge. The human mind which thinks of an ordered structure of power must imagine a centre which provides the centre and the principle of unity of the whole. One supreme being is that centre. But it has to be remembered that his supremacy also has to be considered only 'empirically real'. Transcendantally it has to be 'ideal'. And this in effect was maintained by Shankara, the master founder of "non-dual" or *Advaita* theory of Reality in Indian philosophy.

In keeping with the conception of Brahman, Shankara declared that the One Supreme Being, *Ishwara*, is actually a mental image of Brahman in so far as the human mind can conceive the transcendental absolute at all. So *Ishwara*, the One personal God, the Supreme Ruler of the Universe, though wholly efficacious in the empirical world is conceived of as identical to Brahman. *Ishwara* is immanent as well as transcendent. He is both manifest in time as well as eternal. *Ishwara* is then further equated with the Hindu holy trinity of Brahma-Vishnu-Mahesh each representing the cosmic functions of creating the universe, sustaining it, and finally, at the end of a *Yuga* (a cosmic order of time) dissolving it, respectively. Each is separately represented in a divine human-like form and worshipped in Hindu temples. The Hindu mode of presenting these divine forms in human-like shape naturally yields a number of images of each, according to the imagination of the artist concerned. There is another addition in this presentation. Since the 'power' that *Ishwara* possesses *per se* is also represented independently as females in the embodiment, each primary form of *Ishwara* is associated with a female deity as well. Thus, we have Saraswati with Brahma, Laxmi with Vishnu a:.d Parvati with Mahesh. The worship of these feamle goddesses is most popular all over India. And since in all Hindu worship a concrete image of the deity is used, you can imagine the extraordinary variety in art forms in representing them. Their images are available in all kinds of material giving the respective artist great opportunity of practicing his particular skill. A very large number of artists are involved in this all over the country. Moreover, since an image is a representation of the attributes believed to be possessed by the deity, it gives great opportunity to the artist to image his own form of individuation of the deity. And so, different regions specialise in different forms, giving rise to as rich a culture of all the arts as one can imagine. Indeed it is up to the artist's power of improvisation to imagine meaningfully an image of the deity. Artists involved also include both folk and classical, traditional and modern practices. The result is an ongoing open channel of creativity and a huge cultural industry involving not only temple priests and monks but all the populace in one way or the other.

From the time such a God was introduced in Hinduism, he has remained supreme and other gods have receded into the background This somewhat paradoxical conception of *Ishwara* as 'personal' as well as transcendental is a unique contribution of the Indian mind in the field of religious thought of Reality. Needless to say that it has had a tremendous influence on the cultural outlook. It transformed the popular epistemology of truth as "correspondence" with reality. Truth is now more subject-referring rather than objective and impersonal. It is the human being who can be said to be "in truth" if his empirical consciousness is simultaneously aware of his transcendental background on the model of God who is simultaneously both the impersonal Brahman and the manifest personal God. Truth is now a "mode of being" for the human being within the all-inclusive Reality. Epistemology of a people always has a strong influence on the cultural modes of representing the world. We can see this very clearly when a further novel contribution of Indian spirituality introduces the theory of incarnation.

The doctrine of incarnation has its first clear statement in the *Gita* (though earlier introduced in the *Atharvaveda*). There Krishna is the incarnation of Vishnu. He is addressed as *Bhagavan* which literally means "one who possesses all opulence". With the doctrine of incarnation, the theistic spirituality attains its full glory as the evolutionary expression of man's religious mind. It is original and the single most important contribution of Indian religious experience to mankind. As in all the basic Indian religious thinking, typically it retains its philosophical flavour in an apparently paradoxical conception of the entry of the Eternal into the temporal.

In incarnation God the eternal and the infinitely-infinite Person manifests in the empirically limited quantifiable world of time called *samsara*. In *samsara* all beings have a relative existence, i.e. the same existent is now big and now small, and therefore, all things in themselves are nothing, unreal and impermanent appearances. This is beautifully brought out in *Vaman Avatar* where god appeared in the form of a dwarf in front of a devil-king and asked him for three steps of land which he gave him. But in three steps he measured the whole universe.

The Buddhist spirituality held on to this conception of an unreal Reality and reduced being to nothingness or "no-thingness" or in Sanskrit conceived as "*nissara*". But the Hindus held on to the more positive conception of reality as Being or Brahman, though placing it in the transcendental plane and calling it (within the limits of human mind) "inconceivable". As *Kena Upanishad* puts it: Those who say they know, they know him not, those who know say he is unknowable. We can only touch the boundaries of human thought and think of the power of that which creates the boundary as God. God has to be transcendent as well as relative to the world. This most difficult conception is concretised in the idea of Incarnation: the eternal entering the temporal, the infinite appearing as a finite magnitude and passing beyond the empirical limits into the absolute. In fact, even the incarnation is real only from the relative point of view of *samsara*.

This conception of being and nothingness as two aspects of the divine reality is typical of Indian spirituality. The fullness of Being is also the conception of nothingness, this metaphysical position is well reflected in the Vedic invention of zero as a mathematical quantity, subsequently giving rise to the decimal (*dashamlava*) system of calculation. This product of the Indian mathematical genius is derived from the spiritual insights of the sages. The notion of the divine as infinity has two resolutions.

One, in its positive expression, it is described as *anant* meaning inexhaustible or unending. And the other, in its negative expression, it is described as *anaadi* meaning without a beginning or origin. Being without an origin it is conceived as eternal. And the two infinities combined give the concept of *shunya* or zero. But *shunya* is mathematically a quantity and if it is divided by any determinate quantity it still remains *shunya*. This is the essence of the spiritual reality. It is all and nothing. It is incarnate and describable as well as transcendent and indescribable. God is without an origin and yet related to the world as its creator. God as incarnate is a paradox, an appearance of Reality. Thus in the *Gita* when Arjuna perceives the truth of incarnation he describes Krishna as: Supreme Being, Supreme Abode, Pure, Supreme God...

In sum, it is in the threefold conception of divinity—*Brahman*, *Ishwara* and *Avatar*—and yet integrated in one system, that Hinduism has exercised its most powerful influence upon Indian culture. First, God as Brahman is "One Divine Reality", the ultimate ground of all existence. Next, the Reality may be seen either as Personal God, *Ishwara,* or as *Prakriti*, that is the manifestation of the divine essence in earth, water, fire, air, and space, together with the psychological aspects of Being in thought, intellect and ego. Thirdly, the *Purusha* or the Divine Mind which moves and animates the universe as the indwelling intelligence, is fully displayed in its perfection in the role inacted by the particular person considered to be an incarnation of God. God as incarnate provides the living knowledge of Reality through its most intelligent and creative manifestation in human form. The entire content of God's thought or play-act (*Lila*) is objectified in the universe and pre-eminently in Man. This threefold conception provides the entire range of human understanding of Reality and the entire range of intellectual and emotional possibilities with which man can relate to the divinity in culture.

In this work we will witness very clearly how Hinduism has influenced the Indian culture and helped to answer some of the most important concerns of the Indian society. For example, one very important influence of the spiritual values embodied in Hinduism can be seen in the shaping of modern Indian society after political independence from British rule. India is probably the only post-colonial country which has successfully embraced modern democracy, together with its central values of freedom and the rule of law. It has become a mature, secular democratic state, responsible to international law and justice. The ease with which it has moved into modernity as a whole itself shows that the values of modernity are not an enigma to it. Democracy, for example, requires a sincere respect for other points of view. But it also requires a sense of human equality and ability to live with differences. All these are important ingredients in Hinduism. Hinduism has a living tradition of debate and reasoning on the meanings of scriptural interpretations and on the claims with regard to truth, God, freedom of the individual and so on. This tradition in called *sashtrarth.* When one pundit/scholar or philosopher is defeated in *Sashtrarth* by another pundit of a different viewpoint, his followers also accept the winner's faith.

The Hindu has never used the sword or fear or money to persuade others to accept their viewpoint. Proselytization is foreign to Hinduism. There is total religious freedom and even atheists have their place in the society. It is widely acknowledged that secularism in India exists due to Hindu attitudes. Secularism means that the state should not give patronage to any particular religion. It does not mean that in a democracy no politician should take up issues concerning religious interests. This has been the age-old practice in India as required by Hindu attitudes. Similarly, I hope to show, that when the meaning of culture is properly understood, it will be seen that in other important areas of life, such as education, ethics, social action, and personal human relationships based in love, Hinduism is constantly shaping and improving the Indian culture.

REFERENCES

1. ch. 7, 4.
2. ch. 7, 29.
3. ch. 4, 6-7.

2

A TELEOLOGICAL CONCEPTION OF CULTURE

Lately, Raymond Williams has observed that 'culture' is one of the two or three most complicated words in English language. Yet the word has a very wide currency. Everyone seems to understand it. All forms of social phenomenon seem to have some cultural bias, and their descriptions seem to have some cultural connotations or indirect references. But perhaps the width of its usage, far from signifying a common understanding of the concept, shows a lack of agreement on, and a confusion about, what culture is. In this chapter I suggest an approach towards a definition of culture which if successful would remove some of its complications and render the notion more transparent than what it appears.

Initially, I wish to suggest that the complication arises mainly due to two factors. One is a tendency to conflate the concept with the thing which it picks out and thus to define culture in terms of its products. And the other is to ignore some of the less tangible though central features in the logical behaviour of the concept. I shall discuss three such features, namely, its pluralism, its self-consciousness and its dynamic character.

In its most widely accepted and rather emasculated rendering culture is defined as 'a way of life'. But what is a way of life? In asking this question we are not asking for a description of the contents of a particular way of life; we are asking for those general features in terms of which we can characterize the 'way' part of a way of life. This question puts us immediately on route to the conflation under consideration. For the general features in terms of which we can identify a way of life as such cannot be discovered by empirical investigation. It has to be a philosophical exercise in conceptual exploration. Cultures are radically (indeed notoriously) plural. The all pervading influence of magic, religion or science, for example, constitute very different ways of life. The central features, therefore, in one way of life need not be present at all in another way of life. We are impaled on the following dilemma : either we characterize a way of life in terms of features dominant and peculiar to a particular culture, or we include everything that occurs in a way of life. In the former case culture conceived as a way of life looses its generality, in the latter it looses its distinctive meaning altogether. And in either case it tends to conflate the conceptual contents with the phenomenological contents of culture. I am going to argue that this delimma can be resolved only by taking a teleological perspective upon the subject. That is, an understanding of the concept of culture can come only by way of an investigation of the purpose for which it exists independently of what, as a matter of fact, it tends to produce.

Let us consider the latter form of the dilemma first. On a most general review of the way people live, we can say that human beings everywhere live by way of seeking health, wealth and happiness (in food, shelter, sex, family, friendship, entertainment and such like), but they try to achieve these in different ways attaching values of different weights to their activities. Ignoring those differences for the time being, it appears that a description of the way of life, they adopt in trying to achieve these, would include everything that a people actually did. The word 'culture' would then connote the totality of their activities. The classical statement (still revered) of this position is Tylor's difinition: "... that most complex whole which includes knowledge, belief, art, morals, law, custom, and any other capabilities and habits acquired by man as a member of society."[1] But then, surely the following problem arises. How are we to address those social practices, or traditions of smaller groups, which we consider decadent, and which often thrive, it seems, despite our avowed rejection of them in sincere epistemic, moral or aesthetic evaluations? If culture is all of the manifest life then the expression "cultural degeneration" would seem to have nc application, for the meaning of that expression does not signify undesirable forms of culture but forms of life considered degenerate *from the cultural point of view.* Every society seems to record the menace of certain evil and ugly practices, traditions, attitudes etc., which are often condemned even by those who embrace them, which they wished were not there (like an alcoholic who wishes he did not drink). So if the notion of culture were inclusive, how would we distinguish between what we would like to reject and run down in a way of life and what we would happily uphold? Surely, the norms and standards of such evaluation must come from within the axiological resources of the culture itself. This gives us the suspicion that at the heart of culture lie certain values, standards, ideals which may not find full (or even partial) expression in the real life. Certain practices etc. may crop up from time to time whose geneology could not be traced back to events of specifically cultural recognition. Necessities of survival, for instance, do not necessarily represent cultural demands. By the sheer force of unpredictable and uncontrollable historical events, a community may be coerced into adopting certain lifestyles, certain ways of coping with material emergencies, which is due course of time may produce taboos, rituals and even traditions, which were not intended at the time of the initial adoption of those styles etc. The test of their being compulsions lies in the fact that they are never upheld as steps in cultural progress. The rampant corruption, disorder and confusion in a society, for example, are not necessarily cultural products, though they do indeed suggest a lack of the mechanisms of resistance to corruptibility, in a culture. A culture is often forced to hide the truth about itself. So an attempted definition of culture must be sensitive to its self-assessing, and therefore, self-conscious, normative character. More generally, by virtue of its constitutive involvement with the normative, an indiscriminately inclusive conception of culture will loose its distinctive meaning.

It is this dilemma that lends itself to the unitary notion of culture invoked in the elite ranks of both, the social sciences and the humanities. In this perspective a culture is identified only with what is characteristic or distinctive of a way of life, and, by implication, also considered valuable in it. In the unitary notion of culture what is valuable is the intellectual and artistic product of an elite section of the society, as famously, in Mathew Arnold's words,[2] 'the best that has been thought or known'. From this, it is only a short step to conflate, which is (legitimately) considered distinctive of a culture as a whole. Thus the culture of a complex, class-ridden diversified society may be identified with what is arbitrarily picked out as distinctive of the considered society. T.S. Eliot, for example, says that culture 'includes all the characteristic activities of a people' and then for the British culture he specifies the following items : Derby Day, Henley Regatta, Cowes, the twelfth of August, a cup final, the dog races, the pin-table, the dart board, Wensleydale cheese, boiled cabbage cut into sections, beet root in vinegar, nineteenth century Gothic Churches and the music of Elgar.[3] But from the point of view of an individual of a different class in the same society the list of distinctive items may be considerably different. Thus, for Hanif Kureishi the list of 'characteristic activities' of the British people includes 'yoga exercises, going to Indian restaurants, the music of Bob Marely, the novels of Salman Rushdie, Zen Buddhism, the Hare Krishna temple, as well as the films of Sylvester Stallone, therapy, hamburgers, visits to gay bars, the dole office and the taking of drugs.'[4]

I have taken this comparative example to make the point that the unitary view of culture flies in face of both, the facts and the logic. It is clear that there is no logical way of settling the dispute between Eliot and Kureishi, i.e., of determining exclusively what is characteristic of a way of life of people considered, for example, as one nation or one society. On the other hand, cultures are generally addressed not only on the broad distinction between elite and popular or mass cultures but also in recognition of their variety as developed and backward, African, European and Asian, masculine and feminine, gay, pop, tribal and so on. We are forced to recognize the plurality of cultures, where 'pluralism' refers both to the difference of style as well of thematic meanings of culture activity. Thus even politics is a culture-product where meanings are contested according to thematic differences in lifestyles and cultural interests of different groups. There exists both, the cultural politics and the politics of culture. Once the unitary view of culture is rejected, we are forced to recognize that as it stands 'the way of life' definition does not capture the essence of the matter. In a way of life we can neither include everything that passes in the life of a community nor can we characterize it in terms of what is considered 'characteristic' of it. The way out of this impasse is not, however, to opt for what is known as the super-organic conception of culture. A bold statement of this position declares, "... a culture cannot exist without bodies and minds to flesh it out; but culture is also something both of and beyond the participating members. Its totality is palpably greater than the sum of its parts, for it is superorganic and supraindividual in nature, an entity with a structure, set of processes, and momentum of its own, though clearly not untouched by historical events and socio-economic conditions."[5] From our point of view, however, this definition is also 'inclusive', though culture has been raised to the super organic level of social organizations. Moreover, this metaphysical reification of culture puts it beyond all possible explanation. One cannot even explain how it is "not untouched" by history and society or "fleshed out" by bodies and minds.

The conclusion reached so far—that cultures are self-consciously self-assessive and irresistably plural—gives us a clue to the understanding of the nature of culture. For now, it requires us to understand, not only why certain forms of life are to be considered distinctive of a way of life, but also why what is distincitive is to be considered valuable or significant in a way such that it deserves the title 'culture'. That is, people (communities, tribes) differ considerably in the idiom they employ for the articulation of their meanings, whether that idiom be linguistic, visual, artistic, or whatever, but what is it about them all that makes them cultural? It is clear that the aspect of the cultural cannot consists in the commonality of the concerete items of distinction, nor even in the kinds of ways of articulation of meanings. I am going to suggest that the aspect of the cultural is to be looked for, not in the contents of actual cultures, but in their intentionality, their directedness towards an 'ultimate' meaning—the meaning and purpose of articulating concrete meanings in a variety of idioms. In other words, as noted earlier, understanding of the concept of culture would require placing human life in a teleological scheme, but without the legislative arbitrariness of Natural Law metaphysics. Without a teleological scheme, I will contend, the very point of making the cultural/non-cultural (technical, natural etc.) distinction wilts.

We have seen that the inclusive notion of culture runs into trouble. So does the unitary notion. In a community's life, especially in the complex societies of modernity, different currents seems to run counter or parallel or crisscrossing each other, often signifying independent ways of life. Is, for example, 'consumerism' a way of life or simply a part of a way of life? How would religious fundamentalism or secularism fit into *one* way of life. It is not clear what kinds of patterns of life would constitute a *single* way of life. Other cultural anthropologists attempt to recommend a way of life view of culture seems clearly unsatisfactory. Faced with a bewildering variety of 'scientific' definitions of culture, it will be recalled, Clyde Kuluckhohn and Alfred Kroeber, took upon themselves the gigantic task of evaluating all the current literature available to them on this topic. Having considered 164 definitions of culture under a variety of titles such as, descriptive, normative, psychological, structural, genetic etc., they came to the conclusion that they could identify a common position in all that: "Culture consists of patterns, explicit and implicit, and/or and for behaviour acquired and transmitted by symbols, constituting the distinctive achievements of human groups, including their embodiments in artifacts; the essential core of culture consists of traditional (i.e., historically derived and selected) ideas and especially their attached values; culture systems may, on the one hand, be considered as products of action, on the other as conditioning elements of further action."[6]

This statement is not easy to understand. Different elements in it do not seem to fit well. What is meant, for example, by the talk of "patterns" of behaviour "constituting the distinctive achievements of human groups?" Let us interpret it to mean that patterns of behaviour display the distinctive achievements which are embodied in the intellectual and artistic products of human groups. Understood in this way the definition of culture implied here comes to the elitist conception which we have discussed above, and therefore, suffers from the same defects as the 'way of life'—definitions in general. Moreover, the latter half of the above statement shifts the focus of culture altogether. It declares that cultures consist essentially of traditional ideas and values. But the notion of tradition though incorporates (rightly) the aspect of 'continuity' of cultures, does not necessarily, signify distinctive achievements. As we have already noted some of the traditional ideas and values may not be cultural products at all. They may only reflect compulsions, and in fact may be degenerate. And such traditions in so far as they are seen as 'conditioning elements of further action', must be treated as undesirable continuities. So, if we focus our attention upon the factor of 'distinctive achievements' we are led to the unitary view of culture and if we treat its essential core to be traditions, indiscriminately, we tend to ignore the distinction between specially cultural and accidently conventional or simply convenient and regular. In either case we need to explain why certain distinctive achievements and traditions are to be counted as specifically cultural. And if they are considered, in some sense, perfections of natural human endowments, we need to understand, both, what they are perfective of and why they are considered thus and so. The latter would require us to specify the ultimate goal which the 'achievements' and the traditions are meant to realize—thus bringing into the explanation reference to a teleological scheme of human activity. Moreover, the goal has to be not a merely a dominant aim but inclusive; the good of man's communal, social existence considered as a whole, and not personal, individualistic and idiosyncratic, but something which necessarily requires intersubjective communication for its attainment. Culture is a participatory enterprise of and for the 'whole'.

The lack of such understanding continues to be reflected in more recent approaches to cultural studies as well. Clarke and his colleagues, for example, take culture to be, the way, the forms in which groups "handle" the raw material of their social and material existence.[7] The use of the term "handle" is significant here. It gives a functionalist perspective upon culture. It is the same for some sociologist who see culture as a system of institutions in an organized society. The system is like an engine fitted to a ship, which has to run well irrespective of where the captain wishes to go. But here it is being forgotten that the engine and the ship has to be of a certain type whose nature can be determined only if we know what the captain wishes to do with the ship. This functionalist perspective is better expressed in the idiom of a geographical metaphor which suggests that cultures are 'maps of meaning' through which the world is made intelligible.[8] True, but we should not overemphasize this cognitive function of culture. Culture has something to do with the way these maps are constructed in the first place. Cultures are not inert systems of meanings which we simply consult to find our way about in life. For surely, often quite spontaneously, new ways of making the world intelligible become available to man, which can radically modify the existing 'maps of meaning'—a modification which on the one hand, points to the purposive intentionality of human activity and on the other, to the (all important) dynamic character of culture. Moreover, the inner dynamism of culture is not a mechanical, monotonous, repetitive attempt at reproduction. Rather, it is a qualification of human creativity—of meanings and values. When a culture defined as a system of belief, rules and rituals, skills, practices and traditions, it gives the impression that culture is something static and self-contained—a technology, as it were, for living. No doubt cultures have traditions embodying forms of life and traditions are practices signifying repetitive reproduction of knowledge and values, but robust cultural traditions are open-ended dynamic 'system' of meanings. Their concepts are regulative as well as creative, not a blind alley-way. Cultures have *reason* for continuing to live the way they live, though, unfortunately, in 'closed' and uninquiring societies these 'reasons' are not brought into the open, nor self-consciously discussed and evaluated.

Cultural concepts are always open to fresh interpretations since they are neither exclusive nor wholly transparent. A culture, therefore, must feel justified in its own eyes. This justification cannot come from the built-in 'authority' of cultural traditions themselves, since culture is a field where meanings are contested. Nor can it come from the *de facto* authority of the dominant mode of culture. Cultures, therefore, must be self-consciously self-assessive.

From the conclusions we have reached so far it is clear that an adequate conception of culture must be sensitive to those factors which accounts for its self-consciously normative and dynamic plurality. What is laking in the conceptions we have considered above is the *ratio* or the intelligibility of the large choices which cultural agencies must make, if cultures are to prove meaningful creative realizations of life. In other words, cultures considered as distinctively human enterprise in living could not be represented simply as a way of life. Culture is a *preferred* way of life of a community of self-aware, rational and creative individuals. To be justified in its own eyes, it must have a *ratio* and *ordinatio* of its preferences. And this, once again, requires us to take a teleological perspective upon life. The understanding of a culture, therefore, presupposes some appreciation of how a community views its 'human situation' and in general the character of 'what reality is *for* men' (Hillary Putnam's expression). The teleological perspective involves us, as Alasdair MacIntyre[9] has maintained, in a scheme that links together "man as he is" with "man as he might become, were his *telos* fulfilled." Without a teleological scheme, culture, it seems, looses it significance for life.

Culture embodies those qualities of a community's character and personality which help its people, as a socially organized human group, to fulfil its telos. But where do we look for the telos (or a collective)? To give an account of the telos we will have to, it seems, take recourse to speculative reason and provide an account of human nature based in a philosophy of nature as a whole (as paradigmatically Aristotle did). We would need to know that what according to nature was the goal of human life, which cultures are deemed to realize. But such a view of the human being, as possessing an essential nature and an essential purpose of life, is harly acceptable today. I too hold no brief for that. An acceptable account of the goal of human life will have to be, on the one hand, not too contingent—something which a community simply happens to be pursuing, willy nilly as it were, and on the other, not so uncertain and arbitrary as speculative reason tends to supply. It has to steer clear of these two extremes. But how can we determine a telos by a middle path?

It seems to me that a conception of the telos in question can be arrived at not from the consideration of *human nature* but from the consideration of the *human situation*—a notion which is due to the existentialist thinkers. By *human situation* we mean that primordial relation in which human beings find themselves *vis-a-vis* the all inclusive reality, independently of any metaphysics of how they essentially are. And, surely, it will be generally agreed, that human beings find themselves as essentially nothing ('no-thing' as Sartre puts it), undefined or, to say the least, incomplete, standing in a threatening relationship with the vast unknown ocean of existence.

Now, human life is not a 'given' determinate something. It is being perpetually created in human activity which is purposive and meaningful to those who engage in it. So the life of a community created in inter-subjective participation is a meaningful purposive activity. Culture, as we have seen, is the community's preferred way of life. The direction of life's preferences is set by the primordial relation of man with the unknown. The human being finds himself free to act (his freedom is not *a* being, it is the very being of man—Sartre), but his freedom is haunted by the insecurity of incompleteness. And this situation dictates the telos we are looking for. The human being longs for completeness, for some indefinable totality, comprising of all the generic modes of being available to his consciousness. And culture is that aspect of the life of a community which signifies an on-going *quest* of this completeness or perfection. A quest is a self-conscious engagement with the unknown. Unlike a stagnant culture, a living and progressing culture must be aware of the standards of evaluation of the quality of life that it employs, and being judiciously critical of them, modify, accept or discard them. It will have no justification in employing the standards it does, if they were at the mercy of random historical contigencies. An enlightened culture must at least believe that its standards of evaluation have an ultimate reference to the perfections of human existence.

The best image that man has conjured up of this perfection is the classical 'holy trinity' of truth, goodness and beauty. And though we may have no (as post-modernism will have us believe) historical and theory—independent resolution of the trinity, there is no cause for despair. For to have no agreed determinate concept of the trinity, far from being an obstacle, is a necessary prerequisite for the notion of 'quest' to get a foothold in reality. If what one were looking for were already known, there will be no quest of it as such; there could only be a 'search' for it. But human life being what it is—a launch in the uncharted ocean of existence—its perfections are not and cannot be settled, defined, once for ever. Indeed the human situation is the ideal situation for a quest of life's perfections. The quest is sustained and advanced by its internal logic and axiology, as 'a tradition is sustained and advanced, by its own internal arguments and conflicts.'[10]

We do not have to experience the trinity in advance to have human activity directed towards it. There will be no quest, again, if we know exactly where we were going. There would only be marching 'forward'; and cultures caught up in such marches inevitably lose their creative dynamism and turn degenerate. Life's dynamism consists in its purposive intentionality, in its direction towards a goal which has no finality. This directedness, self-sustaining activity, involving continuing self-assessment and enquiry. It may approach the goal from different directions and in different styles of living. But any serious approach to the trinity would necessarily bring into play its own discipline, i.e., the energy, the passion, the sincerity of commitment to the quest will necessarily involve the community into acting from the background of an integrated scheme of values and virtues, constituting a concrete way of life, and setting a self-perfecting process in motion. For example, no quest of the above mentioned nature can be serious enough without the virtues of sincerity and integrity, and could record progress without the values of freedom, love and understanding.

It follows, therefore, that a way of life will mark cultural superiority if it is well steeped in the quest. Naturally, such a culture will take a holistic view of life and will be deeply involved in understanding the whole of human existence. Needless to say that such cultures will accord a central place to the pursuit of self-knowledge—to the call of Socrates and Buddha to 'know thyself'. Thus, a culture in which traditions are a way of conducting the quest cannot be rigid and insensitive to the wisdom of the 'other'. Its traditions will not wield absolute authority over its people in matters of truth. The authority vested in a cultural tradition, in this perspective, can only be prescriptive not deterministic, and permissive not legislative. It follows from this that a holistic culture, which attempts to unfold the cognitive, moral and the aesthetic truths in one integrated reality is superior to a culture whose approach to live is fragmentary, and which has no, or no integrated, conception of the trinity, and therefore moves meaninglessly and unreflectively from nowhere to nowhere.

True, we have only a formal conception of human perfections, based in our capacity to recognize, negate and transcend the determinate manifest falsities, evils and uglinesses. We recognize them by the familiar pragmatic criterion. In the light of new experiences the false is shed, the ugly and the evil are transcended. We move towards truth, goodness and beauty through negation of these. But for that reason the movement is no less significant. Negation is to the essence of the positive, and the movement through negation is the very dynamism of human existence.

NOTES

1. Tylor, E.B., *Primitive Culture,* John Murray, London, 1871, p. 1.
2. See Mathew Arnold's *Culture and Anarchy : An Essay in Social and Political Criticism,* Smith, Elder: London, 1869.
3. Eliot, T.S., *Notes Towards the Definition of Cutlure,* Faber & Faber, London, 1948, p. 31.
4. Kureishi, H., *Granta,* No. 20, Bradford 1986, pp. 168-69, (*See* also Peter Jackson, *Maps of Meaning,* Unwin Hyman, London, 1989, p. 4).
5. Zelinsky, W., *The Cultural Geography of the United States,* Prentice Hall, New Jersey, 1973, pp. 40-1.
6. Kroeber, A.L. & C. Kluckhohn, *Culture : A Critical Review of Concepts and Definitions,* Cambridge, Mass: Harvard University, 1952, p. 357.
7. Clarke, J. *et al.,* Subcultures, Cultures and Class : A Theoretical Overview in *Resistence Through Rituals,* S. Hall & Henderson, (eds.), Hutchinson Centre for Contemporary Cultural Studies, London, 1976, p. 10.
8. *Ibid.*
9. A. MacIntyre, *After Virtue,* Norte Dame: Notre Dame Press, 1984, p. 156.
10. *Op. cit.,* p. 242.

3

THE INDIVIDUAL AND THE TRADITION

Ever since the beginning of modernity, the new Age of Reason, we have witnessed a steady growth of experimental science, capitalistic economy and, alongside with it, an overpowering cult of Individualsim developing into almost a social ideology. Unfortunately, however, individualism as an ideology, with its focus on the pursuit of self-fulfilment, easily degenerates into egoistic-consumerism undermining the tradition or *parampara.* It has managed to enlarge the area of personal freedom to the extent that the individual seems to have lost all sense of social responsibility traditionally enshrined in *parampara.* In the name of 'untraditional' (a synonym for 'modern') almost anything goes—all kinds of trends, cults and styles. What sort of 'individual' does the cult of individualism presuppose? How free is the individual? What is the meaning of 'individuality'? What is the true nature of *parampara*? Is the rise of individualism necessarily incompatible with respect for tradition? Can an individual grow and realise his human potential without participation in tradition? These are some of the questions that I have tried to answer in this chapter.

Individual, Individuality and Individualism

Behind contemporary individualism lies a notion of the 'self' which originating with Descartes (though he mistakenly identified it with the 'mind') has received considerable philosophical support throughout modernity. In its modified modern form it is the notion that the self is an individual mental substance, simple, indivisible, remaining constant throughout its changing biography. It is an entity which is capable of existing separately from the rest of Being including one's own body. It is no other than the essential 'I', the 'me', the subject of all my experiences. It draws the picture of the individual as a pure egoistic will inhabiting an immortal mental substance. It is easy to see that such a consception of the self easily lends support to the idea of 'personal fulfilment' as the primary goal of life which, in its materialistic version, shades into egoistic consumerism. Are we really such kind of individuals?

In face of the fact that the human being, both in respect of his mind and body, is constantly and unavoidably dependent for his existence upon his immediate environment, which in turn depends upon the interconnectedness of an extraordinarily complex whole, it is difficult to believe that we are essentially, ontologically, separate entities. As we will see shortly, the most widely accepted view of ourselves is a mistaken one. It is a myth promoted by the human desire for an eternal personal existence, itself based in the fear of the 'impermanence of all things'.

Surely 'the individual' as an objective reference point is an actuality. Our human *needs*—physical, psychological and spiritual—constantly refer us to a 'centre' which has to be represented as an entity separate from other similar entities. Again, the unity of consciousness in human experience constantly suggests that I am 'I' and not other thing or person. Our experience of others, though suggests an intersubjectivity, is all pervasively dualistic. Yet at no level of our existence do we encounter substantial separateness. At the most obvious 'bodily' level there is no absolute or ontological gap between the 'I' and the 'We' nor is that so at the mental level. At first it seems obvious that my thoughts and feelings are *essentially* mine: that I give rise to them in some *original* sense, *ab initio.* After all no one else suffers my pain and 'knows' what I am thinking. But phenomenological reflection reveals the truth to be otherwise. The 'ego' far from being the source of 'my' stream of consciousness, is in fact an 'object' of consciousness. We can observe that the 'I' is surreptitiously present with all my states of consciousness. This proves that the 'I-ness' can only be represented as the mode of existence of the states of consciousness—the 'mode' has no existence separate from the object whose mode it is. We can agree then that the individual self, the 'I', is no more than an aspect or an act of consciousness, under which the act in question is considered 'owned'.

When we look at the individual self in terms of its *contents* the message is even clearer. First, in self-awareness we are not aware of ourselves as sort of *things* or entities, simply and uniquely *ourselves.* Rather we are aware of the psychological operations of the 'empirical self' filled with a whole host of mental items supposed to be specific to the individual. In general terms, we ar aware of ourselves as a consciousness, a 'desire to be', directed upon goals of *personal* achievements (wealth or some other form of power: material or immaterial). But where do the contents of the self come from? When we consider the self in terms of its contents—its plans and motives, goals, ambitions and aspirations, fears and anxieties, in short, its 'attachments'—it becomes clear that the 'self' is a cultural product, a psychological construct. At every stage of its life, it draws from the epistemic and axiological resources of the culture to which the individual belongs. During its constitution, the self is *conditioned* in its attachments.

If this is a correct picture of the empirical self—the self who is the actual chooser, the actual antecedent to action—what are we to say of its 'individuality'? The term 'individuality' receives both a quantitative and a qualitative resolution. In respect of the former, we have found that we have no reason to assert the being of a separate individual, an immaterial substantial 'I'. Does it not, then, weaken the claim of one's passions for personal fulfilment in the wake of egoistic consumerism? Does it not destroy the validity of the ideology which puts the 'me' always over and above the 'we'? And does it not also destroy the belief in the 'quantitative' individuality altogether? I think it will be agreed that our response to these apprehensions must be in the positive.

In the 'qualitative' sense 'individuality' is an evaluative term. In involves norms and standards for our choices, our activities, which refer to human freedom—a spiritual quality of the personal-psychological background from which one's choices flow. Now, without going into the positive character of this 'freedom', we can see this much that a person who acts from the inner compulsions of his conditioned self cannot be said to manifest *individuality.* A person who is chained to his attachments would lack spontaneity of consciousness, would lack the background of freedom. The conditioned self cannot act creatively. His actions are better characterised as 'reactions'. We can then safely conclude that the popular ideas about 'individual', 'individuality' and the consequent 'individualism' are mistaken. And that in turn invites a reassessment of the relationship of the individual with tradition.

The Character of Tradition

The advent of modernity in the academic world struck a strong blow to the 'traditional'. Modernity recommended a total banishment of the intellecutal past as enshrined in the Cartesian Methodic Doubt. Everything—all social arrangements, intellectual and scientific enterprises—had to begin with new paradigms. Appeal to Reason was the law, so much so that by the beginning of 20th century 'tradition' and 'traditional' had clearly acquired strong pejorative connotations. But in recent times there seems to be some reaction to this anti-tradition attitude; one often hears the call for a return to traditional values, especially in this country. I believe, however, that this conflicting situation rests on an inadequate understanding of "tradition".

In its most popular (and unenlightened) understanding a tradition is taken to involve practices which are merely repetitive and reproductive or some 'object' (artistic or utilitarian) cherished by the community. Now naturally any reproductive process requires a specific *mode* of production which in turn requires certain skills and virtues in the agent—the individual who 'knows' and practices the art of reproduction. The skills and the virtues refer to the qualities of the individual which are required for the success of his activity. If the object in question continues to be desired over a considerable period of time, the entire practice comes to earn the title 'traditional'. But it does not yet explain the title 'tradition'.

The realisation of the object desired is not the whole explanation of the existence of a tradition. It is generally the case that there lies a goal or purpose to be fulfilled beyond the immediate object desired. This goal or purpose is the culminating *telos* or the tradition. And it is the integrating power of the *telos*-consciousness that renders, what are otherwise diverse, practices/activities with a meaning such that they are seen to belong to one identifiable tradition.

In this teleological perspective tradition signifies an *ordered* 'stream of consciousness' in which generations of experience and knowledge acquired in the pursuit of some human perfection get organised. This stream of consiousness is directed towards the perfection—the *telos*—for whose fulfilment it exists and receives its identity. In traditional knowledge, skills and meanings are enjoined in a goal-directed purposive manner, which otherwise float randomly in the collective unconscious. In a tradition the accumulated 'wisdom' of a community plays a dynamic role by providing an advanced starting point for the younger generation, as well as, by virtue of tis past successes, providing the necessary impetus and inspiration to move towards the *telos*. Thus, a tradition is a dynamic intelligent human phenomenon. One's participation in a tradition is not, and ought not to be, a ritualistic, monotonously repetitive activity. Instead, in a healthy tradition successive generations move steadily and creatively towards the *telos*. A healthy tradition sustains its life in being constantly enriched by new and better ways of realising its *telos*. The more universal its *telos*, the greater the variety in the modes of its realisation. The complex nature of a tradition and the diversity in its practices need not necessarily be problematical, since the role of a universally meaningful and naturally suggested telos is precisely to serve both as *ratio* and the *ordination* of the contents of the tradition.

Traditions can surely degenerate and turn counterproductive. Historically, in face of dangers of survival, smaller units of a community have tended to withdraw themselves from participation in the larger traditions of the society they belong to. Such isolation, social and psychological, produces 'closed' societies, in which the constituent practices of a tradition lose their teleological insights and become simply tokens of community identity. As the emphasis on the easy availability of the traditional object of desire continues, the individual producer begins to work unimaginatively, i.e., carrying on producing the *same thing* in the *same way* with the *same skills* and *virtues*. In this sort of situation the *art* of the practices turns into mechanical routine activity signalling the degeneration of the larger tradition. When this happens we lose sight of the value and the relevance of the particular *mode* of production; it no longer engages the creative consciousness of the producer. The 'artist' no longer feels responsible to improve his skills and personal discipline since he does not see his activity as a creative performance constituted within a broader framework of a tradition.

To take an example let us think of the decay of the traditional joint family under the pressure of modern individualism. Central to the joint family is the practice of sharing the total resources of the family with the members of the family. But the meaning of this practice is not explained simply by the contingent fact that several biologically related individuals happen to be living together; nor is it exhausted by its economic persuasions. Clearly, *sharing* refers to the higher purposes of *caring* for the loved ones, which in turn refers to the moral and spiritual dimensions of human life—of order and compassion, of love and justice—pointing to a universal *telos* which is enshrined in the ideal of our ancient dictum: The World is One Family.

To take another example, consider the practice of painting pictures, within an artistic tradition. It is true that painting pictures is often profitable. It may also be the case that it serves some social purpose and the personal-psychological need of self-expression. But none of these provide a satisfactory explanation of why the practice should be construed within an artistic tradition; why it should continue to be valued when none of these services are rendered by it. Why did the caveman paint, for example? It is believed that the construction of the *Kailash Mandir* in the Ellora caves, carved out of a solid stone hill, took nearly 200 years of sustained effort. Surely such exercises in art cannot be understood without reference to a 'tradition' in a teleological conception.

There is no reason then to treat tradition with contempt, or be pessimistic about it. With a proper understanding of the role of tradition in human life we can see that a tradition has to be innovative or else it would degenerate. In a teleological perspective we can unearth a world of treasures in a tradition and make that our starting point for the innovative strides into the future. We have to realise that for a meaningful 'revolution' we need the background of 'tradition'. A successful revolution is always *within* a tradition and not against it. In a revolution the tradition surpasses the 'givens' of its practices and prepares the ground for a fresh movement with greater intensity and understanding towards its *telos.* In this process it improves upon the very vision of its *telos.*

We can now see that a mindless dedication to the tradition and an emotional rejection of the tradition are both examples of egoistic self-assertion, and not of the 'qualitative' individuality. A real individuality invites a creative engagement with the tradition. In a creative individual choices are made freely and projects are undertaken in the light of full understanding of the meaning of the *telos.* The real individual is not participating in a tradition mechanically with an eye on its utilitarian value alone. Nor is he running away from it. He is not simply reacting from his conditioned background either in conformity or in rejection of the tradition.

The individual's participation in tradition is not an 'optional'. As we have said, the individual self is a culture product; his goals and purposes in life derive from the culture he inhabits. As such he is already rooted in traditions—healthy or degenerate; without tradtiions it would be only by an extraordinary genius or a lucky fluke that he would manage to realise at all, the goods of human life. Taking the teleological perspective the individual must pursue the tradition creatively. Indeed to be able to retrieve our true individuality from the conditioned background of the cultural self we must derive our meanings and be guided by the overriding *telos* or traditions. In this process, while the wealth of the tradition enriches the individual, his creative pursuit of the *telos* enriches the life of the tradition. Thus, it turns out that the individual and the tradition, far from being incompatible, are in fact necessary to each other. The individual whose behaviour is directed simply by the inner compulsions of the cultural self has no real individuality. The real individuality is freedom, *from* the conditioned self, not *for* the self.

4

SPIRITUALITY

I. The Non-Theistic Strand

The Indian spirituality presents itself as a quest of Truth in its ultimate and absolute form. This truth cannot be apprehended as something 'rounded off' as it were, as something which can be brought under a determinate concept or description once for all times to come. It is an open-ended notion, a formal notion, signifying paradoxically perhaps, something which is beyond the grasp of human mind structured in time, something whose very being consists in a constant becoming. This reality is a perpetual process of self-transcendence. Consequently, it is something which can be grapsed only intuitively in a total silence of the mind. This intuitive grasp is itself the generative source of concepts in which the reality is subsequently described. Essentially it is indescribable. Only by recognizing the false as such, in a backward reference, that we move towards the Truth. For this reason, in the strict sense of the word, the Truth cannot be "known", in so far as knowledge comes with a determination of the "given" under concepts. Any conceptual determination of Truth, therefore, must point to a meaning which is beyond it, which every conscious being must apprehend experientially in a phenomenologically transcendental encounter with Reality. Indian spirituality is available in two forms—in a theistic conception and in a non-theistic version. Both forms are interconnected and are still in practice. Both forms are included in modern Hinduism, showing a development from the Vedic Hinduism to the monotheistic Hinduism widely practised today. In keeping with the favous verse in the *Rig Veda* mentioned above, about the "One Divine Reality", gods are recognised only as so many emanations from the One. The classical view about gods is that they are beings inhabiting the cosmos and subordinate to the supreme God. Thus in the *Brahma-Sutra* (1, 3, 26) the various gods appear to have inferior ontological status and religious significance. Thus polytheism is integrated into the structure of a holistic religion. Theism in Hinduism transcends polytheism without rendering it meaningless. Some world religions like Judaism, Christianity and Islam, are strongly anti-polytheism, and hence they are to be distinguished from Indian forms of theism (*see* Ninian Smart, *Doctrine and Argument in Indian Philosophy*, p. 215, London). Let us now see how the story of Indian spirituality unfolds further in both these forms. Indian spirituality, though seems to have existed in pre-Vedic times in Jainism and *Yoga,* received its discursive form in the meditations of the *Vedas* recorded in the *Upanishads. Upanishads* are largely non-theistic, since they set the spiritual task of self-knowledge to the aspirers and the self can be known directly in inner perception only, the worship of a personal god is side-lined as it were. But all along the quest of Truth the reference to the "One Divine Reality" is not lost. And thus we find that the Vedic Hinduism finally introduces the "One" as the original and eternal manifestation of Brahman as a personal God. The significance of this introduction is fully disclosed in the *Gita* and will be discussed later. For the present what is important is to realise that the link with the Vedic One remains unbroken. In his spiritual essence the personal God is identical with the unmanifest eternal Brahman. And the quest of this Brahman is the central aim of the non-theistic spirituality.

The quest of truth culminates in the attainment of a supreme state of spiritual freedom which is the highest essence of Indian spirituality. In its conception this state of freedom has two aspects which are relatively emphasized by different sects. In its more positive aspect it signifies an ascendence into an eternal existence which constitutes a total absorption of the individually constituted self into the universal Brahman. In its other aspect it is, once for all, a freedom from rebirth. The doctrine of rebirth believes that when a human being meets his physical death, he is not spiritually annihilated. His personality surrounding his soul enters the mere body of another living organism and takes a new birth. This cycle of rebirth goes on until his final liberation at the attainment of the spiritual freedom called *Moksha.* The status of his rebirth is determined in accordance with another doctrime of *Karma* which is a causal law applied in the intentional nexus. In its existential manifestations this freedom signifies a freedom from attachment to the individual self constituting one's daily struggles, anxities, fears, loneliness and sorrow. The way to this freedom is the way of self-knowledge. So in order to understand the non-theistic spirituality properly we must understand the concept of the self which is employed by it. We will then be in a position to consider directly how it sees the human condition and its spiritual fulfilment in freedom through self-knowledge.

The Self : A Phenomenological Perspective

In much recent philosophy of the self there are three types of theories which try out what appears to be an exhaustive list of candidates for the position of self-hood. Traditionally the transcedentalists have identified the self with a simple non-material or mental substance while the materialists have identified it with the body endowed with mental attributes. But in between there are theories of the self which treat it as a mental construct negotiated in various ways out of the mental relations stipulated to be occurring in respect of a given body belonging to a person. Traditionally also the understanding of the notion of the self has been sought through the search for the criterion of personal identity. This is so because the self as a personal entity exhibits subjective continuity over time and so, despite its constantly changing biography, whatever is responsible for this continuity, i.e., the criterion of its identity, will also disclose the core properties of selves generally. And further, because the self as the subject of experiences appears to own and unify all the states of consciousness of a person in a single mind. These states otherwise, in the third-person perspective, exist as a mere succession of states. Any theory of the self, therefore, must explain how the phenomenological unity of the self arises.

It is now generally believed that reference to the body alone is unable to explain this unity. Most philosophers, therefore, subscribe to the second or the thrid types of the theories mentioned above. In Buddha's sermons perhaps there is the earliest mention of the self being constituted by putting together of states of consciousness in a string of memories. But he could not explain how memory which is itself a state of consciousness could, as a single occurrent phenomenon, bind all the past, and therefore, presently nonexistent, mental states into one personal consciousness. The problem is that the self is supposed to be presupposed to all the manifestations of consciousness including memories. In modern times, somewhat in the same vein, Hume has given his famous dictum that the 'self is nothing but a bundle of perceptions'; again, not explaining how the otherwise contingently existing separate perceptions come to be united in a single distinct bundle.

All the critereological approaches to the understanding of the self have failed because, among other things, the criterion of personal identity, even if found, could only tell us about the conditions of *sameness* over a period of time; it couldn't enable us to understand what constitutes a person as a self in the first place. The criterion of sameness varies according to the nature of the thing whose identity is in question. The knowledge of the nature of the thing is thus pre-supposed to the determination of the criterion of sameness of the thing. Furthermore the criteriological approach presupposes the validity of the distinction between the 'essential' and the 'inessential' attributes of a thing, and the belief that if a thing retains its essential ones over a period of time then it is the same thing. But there is no general reason to accept either the distinction in question or the belief. If the sameness is defined in terms of the essential properties of the thing then we land into a circularity, for, in face of constant change within substances, the essential itself can be identified only by ascertaining the retention of sameness. In fact 'sameness' is a relative notion—relative to the purpose one has in mind for identifying a thing. If the police is looking for a criminal normally his bodily identity will be sufficient. But if a woman is waiting for her husband to regain consciousness after an accident, then the fact that his brain has been replaced by another person's brain will be a serious matter. Unfortunately, independently of such practical considerations the question 'Is he the same person or not?' has no answer. So how much of what is essential for remaining the same entity over time is a matter of convention or relative to our needs with regard to that person. But identity is a one to one relationship. If A at time t1 is identical with B at time t2 then B has all the attributes of A in all respects of his existence. Clearly such a thing is impossible to determine. The class of 'all attributes of a thing' is an open class. Moreover in case of human beings, it does not even make sense to talk of 'all the attributes', since his creative potential, his moral and intellectual qualities, his self-knowledge and his capacity for subjectivity are all indeterminable factors. Each bout of awareness is existentially new and unique. And, paradoxically perhaps, the possibility of becoming is essential for his being.

Furthermore, in a rough and ready way, one knows that one's identity, in a qualitative sense, changes over time. This is because the memories, intentions, attitudes, prowess etc., which once defined one's identity, become irrelevant, if not totally lost, to one's present identity. Roughly one can say that every so many years one is reconstituted in a new incarnation. But we continue to believe that quantitatively one is the same self as one was as a child. In face of the apparent transformation both in ones' physical and mental composition, one is tempted to believe that what gives unity and continuity to a person is the fact that at root one is a single, indivisible, permanent spiritual entity called the self. But to put the matter in this way rather dogmatically does not provide the criterion of personal identity; it simply asserts that a person is a simple substance and this fact alone is somehow sufficient to explain the unity of mind and the subjective experience of the continuity of oneself.

In our day-to-day life we all employ a concept of the self and along with also a self-concept. The latter refers to my own personal understanding of my character and personality—of who or what I am in my own perception and evaluation. The self-concept has a psychological function in regulating our behaviour. This refers to a largely personal matter and we are not concerned with that in this section. By the former I mean a concept which is implied in the use on all occasions of personal pronouns, but especially the self referring use of the word 'I'. Refernce to oneself in this use signifying self-consciousness at once distinguishes and individuates a single indivdiual entity from among the lot of others, as well as situates it uniquely in the phenomenological ontology of the world. The concept of the self that is implied in these uses gives us the common understanding of what a self is, whose nature can be ascertained by attending to the structure of the ordinary English language in which the concept is exercised, I think it will be generally agreed that in this ordinary conception the self is conceived as a simple indivisible substance, irreducible to other sorts of entities and their relations. Since it is a mental concept its essence is best grasped from the inside in a first-person referential perspective, i.e., in self-consciousness. If that is so then the topic is most ideally amenable to a phenomenological study.

In an analytical study the understanding of the nature of the self is limited to what is believed to be the 'ordinary' concept of the thing. The authenticity of its ordinariness is always in question, partly because we seem to have no clear notion of what counts as 'ordinary' and partly because people differ in the richness which they personally apprehend in the concept.There is always a gap between the concept and the thing to which it applies—a gap which cannot be closed except in case of technical concepts. This gap is easily closed in the phenomenological approach. Phenomenological reflection begins with 'being' which is manifest in the life-world and ends up with capturing the essence encapsulated in the concept. The essential nature of whatever it is to be captures in its pure form, that is, in a form in which the historically accumulated associations which are external to it have been skimmed off. The aim of this enquiry is to conduct this kind of exercise with respect to the concept of the self and thus to test out the validity of the so called ordinary concept in its application in life. It is understood that a revised understanding of the nature of the self will have a profound effect upon our social attitudes and life generally.

Before embarking on the central exercise, however, it is necessary to clear up some popular misgivings about the concept in its many different uses:

1. The empirical self—It is discovered introspectively. It is identified as the Humian 'bundle of perceptions'. But the self is supposed to be that entity to which the whole bundle is allocated. In fact the self is supposed to be responsible for making a bundle out of separate mental states in the first place. It is in the performance of this duty that the self emerges as the *owner* of all one's states of consciousness. It may be the case that the 'owner' in an illusion. But conceptually there is a distinction between the owner and the owned.
2. A third person apprehension of the self is parasitic upon the first-person apprehension. The reason is that understanding "self" as a mental phenomenon cannot be arrived at simply by inference from behaviour, since the latter itself needs interpretation in terms of the mental rather than as a mere happening in the world.
3. In the the Indian spiritual tradition, there is a Self (written with a capital) which is non-egoistic. Strictly speaking it is not a self at all. The self proper is always ego-centred and conscious of its indivisibility, singularity and separateness. The 'big' self is a kind of "ground of being". It is universal as opposed to the individual.
4. The divide between the self and self is not the same as between the empirical self and the transcendental self. The latter retains its individuality and separateness even in transcendence.
5. The notion of pure ego representing the transcendental self is hard to understand. Given that a self is always a subject of experiences, it is difficult to imagine a self transcendent to all experiences.
6. "Self-consciousness" does not signify a cognitive relationship between the knower-self and the known-self. It is

better described as 'consciousness of consciousness' where the former consciousness signifies, as Sartre puts it, the awareness that "I am not that thing of which I am conscious".

7. In self-awareness one apprehends oneself as an embodied being. The body is given to me as the subjectival centre for my point of view upon the world. It is not given to me like an object with which I am only externally related. But this leads to a paradox: Consciousness says to itself "I am this" where "this" refers to a particular body. But in the very saying of it consciousness distinguishes itself from that particular body. Self-awareness is thus double-edged. It is simultaneously both identity and distinction from a particular body. This paradoxical nature of self-awareness should warn us from rushing to identify the self with an individual mental substance.

With the above qualifications in mind, we can now proceed with our enquiry. The first thing to note is that since self-awareness does not signify a cognitive relationship between a subject and an object, our inquiry into the nature of the self has to take a detour. We see that the self is not 'given' as an independent entity with its own phenomenological properties. There is no unique property of an "I-ness", nor does being a self feel like anything in particular. So the right answer about what a self is, has to be sought indirectly, *via* the inquiry into what is involved in possessing self-consciousness, recognising the fact that there is no self antecedent to self-consciousness. Obviously it makes no sense to think of selves as 'lying around' as it were, without being engaged in the act of "owning" experiences which are ascribed to them. And the ascription of mental states to selves cannot be held in the same way as the ascription of properties to material objects. It has to be an act of a kind of 'owning-consciousness'.

Now, since the self is supposed to be the subject of experiences, the question about what is involved in self-consciousness amounts to a question abount what is involved in "having experiences". How, for example, it is different from the occurrence of an un-owned experience-sequence identified in relation to a particular human body? Some philosophers would not buy the idea of unowned experiences at all. But must experiences be had by some entity which in itself remains unchanged and the same, while experiences come and go through it, as it were? Will that kind of relationship between the entity in question and experiences be characterised as "having" of experiences? Phenomenological reflection reveals otherwise. At the ground level of experiencing, the experiencer is wholly coeval with his experiences. There is no ontological gap between the two. When I experience pain, for example, if I confine my atention exclusively to the sensation, I find that I have 'become' pain through and through. In the 'experiencing' *per se,* there is no 'I' assigning the pain to itself. But immediately after each moment in experiencing, there is a reaction of 'thought', saying "I am in pain". It is in this reaction that the "I" arises. Thought always divides experiencing into the subject and the object of experience. Experiencing in itself is 'whole', without an experiencer. But thought apprehends it as a relation. So it is clear that the moment to moment occurrence of 'experiencing' is being followed by a running commentry by thought. And the experiencing-self exists in the commentary only. It is a product of thought and, for that matter, an after-thought. That is, when Consciousness is fully immersed in having experiences, there is no 'extra' input by the subject which may account for the 'having-aspect' of his experiencing-consciousness. In reality there seems to be no difference between the occurrence of 'experiencing' and the so called 'having' of experiences. The notion that the 'experiencing' is something which an independently existing self, an experiencer, is having seems to be otiose. The conclusion thus arrived at can be confirmed in ordinary experience, especially in deep creativity, when the actor is completely absorbed in his activity, and there is no consciousness of a separate doer or creator. It shows that 'having experiences' does not signify an "external" relation between the self and the experiences it is supposed to be having.

We have said that the reflective thought divides experiencing into the experiencer and the experience. Let us now see what conscious mechanism is involved in this process. I will call it the "double intentionality" of thought-consciousness. On the one hand, like all acts of consciousness, thought is directed towards an 'object' (which need not exist in *rerun*), and simultaneously, the thought-act is also directed, in a back-firing as it were, towards the source of itself, the 'thinker' giving rise to itself, with the difference, that the backward intentional object is ever inexistent. This double reference of intentionality, not recognized by Brentano, is natural to all thought-acts, in which concepts are exercised in recognition of the experiencing-consciousness. Perhaps the following analogy will clarify the point. Imagine an arrow in flight. When one is aware of an arrow in flight, one is, in the same instance, aware of two essential features of its character as movement— One is the forward directedness of the arrow towards its target, and the other is the same movement signifying the arrow's getting away from the place of its origin. Both ideas are included in the awareness of the arrow in flight. In a like manner, a sudden appearance of a thought in consciousness, signifying a movement in the intentional nexus, includes both, the consciousness, signifying a movement in the intentional nexus, includes both, the consciousness of its directedness towards an object and the consciousness of its separation from a place of its origin. And since the occurrence of a thought is seen as an act, the 'place' of its origin is seen as an agency, which is subsequently identified as the self. It is important to remember that no phenomenological property in the thought itself discloses the nature of the agency. This proves the point that self-consciousness is given to us as a non-cognitive aspect of *thought* under which it is considered deliberated by a wholly independent entity called the self.

All the same, it must be admitted that we do carry a sense of continuity through time, a feeling of being the same self from childhood to the present. How is this to be explained within the account of the self we have arrived at? It seems to me that the perceptual mind is constantly in a state of "recognising-consciousness". Every perception is automatically interpreted in terms of relevant past impressions incorporated in the concepts exercised in recognising the given perception in the present. Thus, the conceptual exercise performed in recognition has always an implicit reference to a personal past in which the concepts were originally learnt. Since recognition is a species of thinking, it always carries a self-awareness, as an aspect, as we have seen, of the thought under which the thought is considered owned. Now, when a fresh thought arises in such a background, there is a co-occurrence of the self-aspects of the fresh thought and the background-thought. It is this phenomenon of the co-occurrence of self-consciousness that seems to produce the feeling of continuity which we carry throughout our lives.

Let me quickly sum up the conclusions so far and confirm what we have learnt about the nature of the self. Since we cannot take a cognitive perspective upon the self, we can know about it only from the phenomenon of self-consciousness. In that we found that the consciousness of the self arises only in the divisive action of reflective thought commenting on the spontaneous ground-level experiencing-consciousness. There is no consciousness of a substantial self-entity. Further, the feeling of continuity through time of a substantial self is an illusion. We are now in a position to conduct the exercise of a phenomenological reduction of "self-consciousness" itself. If we subtract all the historically associated and culturally constituted attributes of the self from self-awareness, together with the illusory feeling of temporal continuity, we are left with only a pure "being-consciousness". This being-consciousness is not the consciousness of *a* being. It has no phenomenological properties. Nor does it have any temporal boundaries. It is simply the 'ground' for the historical self-consciousness, and in that sense, it can be called the "essence" of self-consciousness, and perhaps the ground of all phenomenological consciousness. Being-consciousness is not intentional, not directed upon anything, nor it is originating from anything. In that sense it is *causa-sui.* Needless to say, it cannot be a matter of conceptual awareness. It can only be an original disclosure of being *qua* consciousness.

From the above discussion of the phenomenon of self-consciousness, it is clear that the spirituality centring around self-knowledge distinguishes between the Ordinary individual self, philosophically called the empirical self, and the transcendental ground of this phenomenon in pure being-consciousness. The latter in the Hindu tradition is called Brahman and a mystical encounter with Brahman is considered as the supreme spiritual experience. The individual self, as we have seen, turns out to be only a mental construct created out of the various experiences of life, most importantly unconscious 'memories' deposited in the brain. The individual self-hood, therefore, has no permanent significance, and in that sense it offers an illusion of continuity of the self-same person. In the mystical experience of Brahman the individual self withers away. Only the all-pervading, everlasting Brahman is ultimately real.

So in the non-theistic spirituality, self-knowledge or self-realization means the same as the direct, non-discursive, experiential knowledge of Brahman. Typically, in this strand of spirituality, it is claimed that this knowledge can be attained without recourse to the knowledge of a personal God. Thus theism is essentially irrelevant to this enterprise. Traditionally contemplative *Yoga* has been considered as important method of accessing the Brahman. The essence of *Yoga* is to attain a total "stillness of the movements of consciousness". In this state, when thought process is completely suspended, Brahman is revealed as a universal creative force behind the universe. The experience of this reality is variously described by the self-relised saints, with the caution that no description ever significantly captures the Truth, as it is stated in the famous apothem that "Truth is one but the learned speak of it variously".

The other less ascetic approach to self-knowledge is the method of spiritual "enquiry". In modern times Raman Maharshi has been a well known exponent of this method. In this, one asks oneself the question, "Who am I?" But this asking is not a mere intellectual exercise, as it is not for the knowledge fo the historical identity of the enquirer. Rather, in an inward intentionality, and in total attention to what is going on experientially, the enquirer penetrates the deeper layers of the mind eventually entering the timeless eternity. In the rapt attention of a sincere enquiry, the mind attains, quite spontaneously, the stillness which the ascetic *Yogi* achieves with skilful efforts in harnessing the "modifications of consciousness". Essentially, the enquirer tries to get to the very core of his being by separating his bodily and mental identies from the pure being-consciousness. The enquirer perceives directly that he is not the body with which he identifies himself. Further, he perceives that he is not the ephemeral states of consciousness which rise and fall in him independently of his will. He is simply a "witness" to all the phenomenal reality he normally identifies with. Raman Maharshi discovered that in the end he was simply the pure "Universal Self" with no trace of an individual ego. This was Brahman, beyond the conception of a personal God.

In somewhat the same vein, a more recent spiritual teacher, J. Krishnamurti, has also maintained that self-knowledge is the key to the attainment of the highest state of truth. But he differs from the tradition in his approach to it. He rejects all forms of imposed discipline or 'method' to be practised to get there. His claim is that self-knowledge accrues upon one in the understanding of the day-to-day ordinary relationships which surround a person—his relationships with things and people and even with ideals and dogmas. This understanding can take place if, in "choiceless awareness", a person remains watchful of all the activities and conscious states which he engages in. This silent, non-cognitive, self-awareness discloses to the person the hidden motivational structures of his personality—his fears, anxieties, greeds etc.—and leads him, again, quite effectlessly, into a total understanding of himself—of how he is psychologically constituted and why does he live the way he does, in relentless struggle, conflict and sorrow. This self-understanding, Krishnamurti tells us, naturally produces a spiritual "silence" in which the ultimate, the eternal, the "nameless" is spontaneously revealed to the aspirant. So again the emphasis is on 'discovering' the truth without a prior commitment to a particular conceptualized faith.

All the same in the Hindu tradition, some non-theistic seekers of Brahman admit the existence of a personal God but limit his gracious significance only to being a teacher and a guide, and in that sense a helper. According to them the personal God at the most can give you the strength to pursue your spiritual enquiry, but he cannot give you the Enlightenment itself. The non-theistic spirituality is hard to embrace, and naturally most Hindus follow the theistic path. But the ideal of independent enquiry and faith in the unaided capacity of man to reach out to the highest has deeply influenced the Hindu culture. In the heart of hearts everyone believes that in the end the individual has to depend upon himself. The non-theistic spirituality glorifies humanity and upholds the truth that the human being is the true beginning and end of all human endeavours.

II. Theistic Spirituality

The Project of Freedom in Theistic Spirituality

The cenral ideas of non-theistic spirituality, introduced in the *Rig Veda* is that Being is "one divine reality" and the idea introduced in the *Upanishads* that the individual is basically of the same essence as that Reality was never given up. This conception set the project of freedom of consciousness. The freedom of *Moksha* consisted in a conscious self-realisation of this sameness of the essences of the divine reality or Brahman and the individual or the *Atman*. Now with the introduction of a personal God, *Ishwara*, the formless Brahman is seen to assume form as the original manifestation of Brahman as consciousness with the power of "thought" called *Adideva*. The goal of freedom still remains the same. But a new mode of access to the divinity, a new approach in the quest of *Moksha* comes into being. It is worship, comprising of meditation, contemplation, chanting of divine names, singing and dancing in the ecstasy of love of *Ishwara* and in the pinnacle state of this process experiencing the presence of the divine form filling one's entire being and eventually merging one's individual consciousness in the universal consciousness of the divinity.

This principle was philosophically stated by the philosopher-saint named Shankara whose discourse is known as *Advaita Vedanta* and who enunciates the central principle as follows:

> Brahman is Real
> The 'world' is a myth
> The individual soul (*jivà*)
> And Brahman are not distinct

He explains it analogically that like a wave disintegrates in the ocean and becomes one with it, the self-realized worshipper of God attains the divine consciousness of "Being, pure consciousness and bliss". In theistic Hindu spirituality, great importance is given to the musical dimension of worship. What is known as *sangkirtan* comprising of singing devotional songs, rhythmical singing and dancing etc. together, is culturally most significant. It can involve smaller groups as well as a whole community. And wandering monks, like the famous Chaitanya of Bengal whose *sangkirtan* centres around their devotion to the incarnations of Rama and Krishna mainly are still frequently seen. It is a social form of worship, often encouraging musical forms of very high quality. In the Sikh temples, for example, their *shabad* devotional singing is completely cast in the classical notes of *Ragas* most of which were written by the great guru Nanak himself. In most Hindu temples all over India some *Sangkirtan* is performed regularly. There is no organised compulsion to attend these gatherings—but people in large numbers attend these as and when they feel inspired to do so. The great musicians known as Tyagaraja of South India and Bhatkande of the North, who gave notational structure to the classical musics of the South and North respectively, were both saints who sang their way to God in worship.

The enormous influence of theistic spirituality on our musical culture is so vivid that we do not generally realise it as such. The ragas which have served as the foundation of Indian music for thousands of years originated in the Vedic period in the singing of hymns as a part of early worship of gods. The invocations which were recited, which are believed to possess supernatural powers in their sounds, which are known as *mantras*, are actually musical. Their powers came from the fact that the vibrations and their resonances produced by singing the notes in their purity in particular arrangements of the notes, in total harmony sensitive to the structure of time between the notes; produced characteristic natural effects in the environment.

Thus it is popularly known that the 16th century vocalists named Baiju Bavara and Tansen, demonstrated several effects in the royal court of Akbar, including the lighting-up of candles by singing *Deepak raga* and causing rain by singing the well-known and highly sophisticated raga called *Megh Malhar.* The influence of the insights of *Sama Veda* upon music is so profound that all the later developments are evolutions from the Vedic core. Two modern lines of evolution need special mention. In the middle ages their arose a kind of singing called *Bhajan*. These quickly became extremely popular and spread across India mainly because they were sung by wandering monks. These are devotional songs and they are until today found in every home in India. In fact, the more so today, due to their availability on electronic media. The other tradition is more recent. It is popularly known as 'film music'. The enormous number and popularity of Indian movies is well known. What is interesting to note is that all their so called 'popular' songs are still rooted in the traditional *ragas*. Although they are different in the styles of singing, the experts can detect the underpinning of classical ragas. Because of the nature of its source the Indian music still retains an extraordinary spiritual quality in its harmony embodied in its traditions of freedom of improvisation within a total control of the rythmns of the beats, freely flowing in a melody which is constantly self-transcending.

The Doctrine of Incarnation and its Cultural Significance

The doctrine of incarnation which was first propounded in the *Gita*, brings a totally new perspective in theistic spirituality. The Indian vision of truth of Brahman, is that of a sacred reality which constitutes a sense of connectivity with all the forces of the cosmos. The human being has a special place in it since he is endowed with the capacity of intuition of this reality and his own connectivity with it. In addition, he has the power of creativity, which is his freedom, and his power of imagination to enable him to shape his own destiny. God's incarnation is a proof of this connectivity with the 'one divine reality' refered to in the Vedas. So, there is a continuity from the formless Brahman to the concrete divinity in the form of a human being himself. Spiritually, incarnation or *avatar* as it is called, refers to a deeper reality in human nature. It is connected with the possibility of experiencing a range of emotions without which typically human life, considered as a whole, is incomprehensible.

Emotions on the other hand cannot be understood without their manifestations in human beings. Think of a smile and the emotion it carries beind it, and now try to think of a smile without a human face. It is not possible to imagine or communicate emotions without the embodiment of the soul. And perhaps it is also not possible to communicate spiritual thoughts without a bodily involvement. So perhaps the Arch Angel Gabriel had to appear in human form in order to communicate the holy Quran to Muhammad. Now belief in a personal God requires that we are able to communicate with Him on a person to person level. How can we do this if God has never assumed a human embodiment? A worshipper asks for grace from God. He imagines God with moral and other attributes of the Beautiful. He thinks of God with other psychological attributes such as mercy, compassion, kindness, forgiving and so on, and the one who listens to his prayers. All these relationships with God involve emotions. He cannot pray to the formless Absolute and seek a relationship with it. God's *Avatar* enables Him to show in a concrete way that He cares for man who can relate to him as a human being would do to another. Moreover, God can communicate directly to mankind. This purpose is clearly stated in the *Gita*: "Whenever there is great decline of *dharma*, I incarnate to communicate the Truth to mankind, and to remove the cause of *Adharma* from the earth."[1]

We have seen in the previous section that in principle everyman has the capacity to find Truth by himself. But life being what it is, the conditioning of ages through various rebirths, and of the present life in our childhood, most of us have lost the motivation to search for Truth on our own. Even if we are circumstancially lucky enough to be rightly motivated, we are unable to discern the right path. And again even if we are able to see the right path, we lack the initial energy to move along the path. For all these reasons we need God's grace. Avatar makes it all possible. God who walks amongst men shows us the right path directly, and shows us the path of love of God or *Bhakti* through His relationship with them. He teaches us what the Truth is and how to receive it with his grace. In a gracious advice to Arjuna Krishna says:[2]

Refusing all recognised ways of right and wrong
Come to my refuge alone
And I shall destroy all your sins
And give you the Eternal Freedom

And then to assure him firmly Krishna gives him the "vision" of his divine nature and of his original emanation for Brahman. Thus the purpose of incarnation is realised since the Truth is revealed to mankind and the way of receiving *Moksha* is declared. The whole episode of *Avatar* turns the otherwise meaningless-appearing life and the material universe into a meaningful whole. Life has a purpose, which is to realize its spiritual end of *Moksha*. And God is both, the abode and the way to *Moksha*. Man can find Truth through devotion to God in one of his incarnate forms. When devotion is based on the concept of a messenger, it necessarily becomes more formal. As one contemporary saint puts it: "the *bhaktas* and *sufis* were more comfortable with the idea of *Avatar*. For an intimate relationship, God comes directly. Your love for God becomes authentic when you are assured of his love for you. In the *Bhagvad Gita* it is Krishna who first tells Arjuna "you are dear to me" which enabled Arjuna to surrender." (Sri Sri Ravishankar, *Times of India*, p. 14, 25.10.03)

According to *Samkhya* and *Yoga* philosophy *Avatar* proves the descent of *Purusha* or pure intelligence in *Prakriti* or nature. The world exists by the union of the two. In a way each one of us is like an *Avatar*, because the pure intelligence of the human soul is implicated in the order of nature. The only difference between God's *Avatar* and the human being is that God knows who he is and what is the purpose of his involvement in the world, while man is ignorant of his origin. The phenomenon of incarnation serves first to remind man of his origin and then to encourage him to return to it. The whole episode of God's appearance on earth introduces a new epistemic category in human understanding of the ultimate truth. It is the category of "faith". Faith is to be distinguished from blind belief. Nor is it something arrived at by discursive reasoning, or belief based in the authority of another man believed to be God's messenger. How do we know that someone is a messenger in the first place? For that we require faith in the beginning and the whole exercise becomes circular. But in *Avatar* we are confronted directly with the immense power of God, who in spite of it, in order to provide an ideal to human beings,uses it discretely only to destroy such evil which cannot be erradicated by most efficient human effort alone. Thus in the epics of *Ramayana* and *Mahabharata* we find that all the devils destroyed by Rama and Krishna are endowed with supernatural powers as boons earned by pennance and worship of various gods. As a result, when they turn hostile to humans they cannot be destroyed without divine intervention. And *Avatar* fulfils this function which God performs with due regard for moral and natural laws. The value of faith is fully displayed and justified during the drama inacted in Avatar. Thus faith has reference to relevant experiences in real life. Faith is a holistic category of knowledge which is arrived at by a sincere seeker of truth through the involvement of his whole being. In faith intuition is built upon intimations of divine presence in experience.

The doctrine of incarnation brings with it a whole gamut of concepts which in their existential import have exercised a profound influence upon Indian culture. It introduces a completely new set of values in personal and social relationships, together with a new set of moral values which exist only in developed cultures. In the *Gita,* Krishna introduces a completely new notion of "acting without expecting a personal reward in return". This means that from the agent's point of view when he undertakes to do something good and worthwhile, inwardly, in his psychology, he is completely detached from the idea of personal gain through that action. He acts from the love of the act or simply from the sense of doing something good and beautiful. This notion of "selflessness" in action subsequently becomes the corner stone of Indian culture because of its existential manifestations both in social and personal relationships. In personal relationship it manifests as an ideal of "love". From now on love, as we will see in a later chapter, has to be free from the desire of reciprocity. The lover is not to expect love or any other material rewards in return for his love. This notion of pure love, though hard to practice, remains an ideal till today. All kinds of literature write about it. Music sings about it and art portrays it in its own media. Its spiritual origin is fully recognized in Indian society. And scriptual and religious traditions speak of it as the only true conception of love. The same comment applies to the widening of the scope of morality to include not only the members of one's own kin but the whole of mankind. It is in fact the practical application of the principle of justice with total impartiality. In the *Gita*, Krishna's teachings are set in this context. In the battle of Kurukshetra, Krishna is backing Arjuna, who is to fight out his reigning cousins. Kauravas, for his share of the kingdom, forcibly and immorally taken away from him and his brothers by Kauravas. Kauravas are supported in the battle by many of the elders of Arjuna as well as his teachers and loved one's because of their commitment to the throne they are serving. Now in the battlefield when both sides are facing each other and the war is about to begin, Arjuna is struck by sorrow and lamentation. Seeing that he has to kill his elders and teachers etc. Arjuna is grieved and declares that he will not fight for the kingdom when it involves killing his kinsmen, elders and teachers. At this point Krishna, widening the scope of morality, invokes the principle of universal application of the moral law. He tells Arjuna that he would be failing his duty if he didn't fight, since he was fighting for justice and not for personal gain. All those who are on the side of evil for whatever reason they may be, have to die. In this way the scope of morality was universalized by Krishna in a real life situation. In general the whole life of Krishna provides a role model for every stage of the life of ordinary people. The epics, narrated in great detail teach us the archetypal essences of humanity. Again in the social field the idea of total selfless service is very powerful. Though a social good-doer may in actual fact receive rewards and recognition, he is not to demand it or even expect it.

Today hundreds and thousands of social volunteer groups, organised around some or other saint of some or other religion, are working in the country who are guided by this ancient principle of 'selflessness' introduced in the *Gita*.

In the field of morality we find that the concept of selflessness has a fundamental contribution to make. It comes about in the following way. We know from the academic discourses in modern moral philosophy systems that there is a kind of crisis in ethics as a whole. Ethics or morality is supposed to be 'autonomous'. Surely, if my being moral is based in prudential reasons then it is not being moral as such. Similarly, if the practice of a virtue is ultimately for personal gain then it is not virtuous. This much will be agreed by everyone. But how does one justify its autonomous status? Any justification would need its founding on something which is an ultimate 'end' for human life, which does not need any further justification. Now the Indian spirituality provides this by its reference to the concept of selflessness. As we have seen in the previous section, selflessness when interpreted in terms of inner transcendance is the ultimate spiritual condition of a man who has found truth. Such a self-realised person who has attained freedom from self sees everyone 'in' God and God 'in' everyone. So, selflessness represents a condition with two sides to it, as it were. Looking at it spiritually, it is 'freedom', and looking at it morally it is total non-attachment to personal gains. Such a person doesn't need moral guidance from ready made principles, for he always responds from the point of view of general happiness. In such a person morality and spirituality coalesce. In other words, spirituality, that is reference to the sacred, provides the foundation for morality. Morality is not derived from any spiritual principle, it is itself a spiritual principle. In this way, morality is an ultimate end of life and, therefore, it can be safely treated as autonomous. In Indian culture ethics and spirituality are not separate compartments of life. Rather, virtue is the principle of unity of life.

The doctrine of incarnation has further infused Indian thinking with religious notions which have great significance for personal relationship. The notion of 'faith', in the divine presence in relationship, imparts a sense of sacredness to the loving relationship of mankind. The faithful is never forgotten by God thus a sense of loyalty with honour is also introduced in the cultural stream. Faith brings with it the all important notion of 'trust' and personal 'integrity' of the trustworthy. The whole social life is touched with a feeling of sacredness.

The general message of incarnation is that hedonism and utilitarianism are inferior to love. All social and moral relationships should be based on love. Only then they remain incorruptible. The Vedic insight that 'the world is one family' has the divine backing of the incarnate God. It is not simply a brute fact of evolutionary anthropology that humans seek each other and fulfilment comes through sharing and caring. The intentional nexus of human life is derived from the fact that God, the eternal Person is the creator and sustainer of life on earth. The incarnate God guarantees this truth. He is caring and forgiving and engaging for one who is willing to take it the way it is.

Lastly, a most important characteristic of this spirituality is its connectedness with the entire past. It portrays a magnificent unbroken evolutionary synthesis of ideas as old as the written word itself. From the *Rig Vedic* non-theistic notion of 'One Divine Reality' to Supreme Being as personal God to its various incarnations in many different forms, destroys all the ideological constraints with which many religions suffocate. There is One in Many and Many in One. It explains the Indian sense of tolerance for the diversity of religious views. When God himself assumes many forms and appears among humans in different ages and cultures, then how can there be intolerance for something new or different! All modes of worship, all forms of access to the divine are permitted. Hinduism, strictly speaking, is not one monolithic construction. It is a whole civilisation spread across time and diverse peoples with a tremendous urge to access truth in all its endless manifestations. That is why Hinduism is so colourful and full of life and infinite freedom. Not simply freedom of worship and freedom of religion, but 'free worship' and 'free religion', is the message of Indian culture. All its festivals stand for the celebration of life and living together. The spirit behind it is tremendous and love is the colour of life.

Finally, the Indian idea that creativity is inherent in human nature, and exercising it signifies participation in the spontaneous expression of divine nature, is fundamental to the arts. On the one hand, artistic practice has the virtue of earning merit for the improvement of destiny in the next life. On the other hand, the practice of creativity in any form is considered a form of devotion to God. Through creativity, therefore, one can ultimately reach out to God himself and attain the final liberation or *Moksha*. So, unlike merely secular conception of art, all art is sacred. This spiritual dimension of art opens up infinite possibilities of improvising forms and meanings. It introduces an openness in the arts, and gives the artist the status of a free man. It is this feature that provides the ontological basis for the sanctity and dignity of human life itself. Secular art is dependent on the derivation of sensual pleasure and worldly gains of wealth and recognition etc. But when art is practiced with its sacred reference it becomes the source of true joy and happiness which is different from mere pleasure. Art then becomes an end in itself and a primary fulfilment of human existence.

NOTES

1. *Gita*, Chapter 1, 30-33.
2. *Gita*, Chapter, 18, 66.

5

TRANSFORMING THE HUMAN CONDITION

Surely all philosophy at root must be a quest of truth, which is consequent upon knowledge of 'what is'. And if knowledge can be classified, in terms of its significance for human existence as a whole, as higher and lower, corresponding to its inclusive and comprehensive character, then philosophy ultimately must be concerned with the highest Truth. This quest actually exists and in some form or another it has existed since antiquity. This fact itself points to something characteristic of the human condition—it is the emergence of knowledge in the human being and the revelation of his own reality through it. Knowledge in the phenomenological perspective is something that *happens* to a human being, and though cultural factors may influence its constitution at macro level, it cannot be the case that it is initially, wholly and deliberately socially constituted. When it *happens* consciousness is lit up with meaning. First consciousness is presented with "being such" or "what is" without knowledge of the 'what' of the being. Then subsuming the 'given' under concepts, though an active process, takes place automatically as a reaction of memory, and thus the knowledge born of it is still inert, 'just there', unconscious. But fortunately another lighting up takes place. Consciousness realizes that it is conscious of a reality. And simultaneously it becomes self-conscious. This conciousness of consciousness, as described in his phenomenological ontology by Sartre, is "consciousness that it is not that thing of which it is conscious". In his terminology, consciousness is not *a* being. It is not *something,* though it is not nothing. In a hermenutical interpretation we can say that it is a 'no-thing'. This points to an important truth about human beings—they are not 'finished products', closed systems and therefore wholly determined. This piece of self-knowledge assures us that at the heart of human beings there is freedom. And freedom is power to shape oneself as conscious beings—a power which is built into their mode of being in the world. This gives a clue to an initial characterization of the human condition in his situation, that, basically it could not be a static phenomenon, since some human beings at some or other time must have exercised their freedom and influenced the human condition generally. There is another more important epistemic fall out of this bit of self knowledge. The second lighting up that I mentioned earlier sets up a parallel processing apparatus, as it were, empowering us with an awareness of the distinction, though not the criterion, between truth and non-truth. When I realize that I perceive something to be thus and son, then only, the scepticism that perhaps it is not so can find a foot-hold in reality. One realizes that all that glitters is not gold. Another point of importance is that since consciousness can be perceived only in a non-cognitive awareness, the self cannot be given as an object of consciousness. The self can be apprehended only in relationship with other objects of perception, as each act of consciousness turns upon itself revealing the knower only as an aspect of the act under which the act appears to be 'owned' by an independent agent. But in the phenomenal reality the owner is inseparable from the act, the consciousness is inseprable from the cognizer.

However, this general perception of the human condition must be fleshed out with its phenomenological manifestations in its dynamic modes of existence. Though no doubt, certain features in the human situation can be identified as having persisted throughout the course of history, which have conditioned existence pervasively, and in that sense they are universals, but the mechanism by which they enter the human situation in the first place remains hidden. The phenomenon of being human in the lived and the perceived world is constantly being defined and redefined through culture. But we need to know the interface between the transcendental and the empirical, the eternal and the temporal, the material and the spiritual, which constantly bridges the gaps between them, and makes the former relevant to the latter accordingly.

I am inclined to take my clue from a prayer recorded in the ancient text of *Brihadaranyaka Upanishad* (I, 3, 28) which reads as follows:

> Lead us from what IS NOT to what IS
> Lead us from Darkness to Light
> Lead us from Mortality to Immortality.

Since a prayer is meant for everyone, we can safely assume that in each line the Vedic seers first state their perception of the human condition, and then pray to be led out of that into a condition which accords with their image of the human perfection. Let us look at each of them in their symbolic accretions and see what the human condition looks like in its existential contents.

In the first, the IS NOT is about Falsity, Appearance, Lack, Delusion and Evil. The IS is about Truth, Reality, Sufficiency, Substantiality and Goodness. In the second prayer, Darkness is about Ignorance, Confinement, Dependence, Sorrow an Limit. And Light, though receives a wide interpretation, is essentially about Enlightenment, Expansion, Power, Bliss and Cosmic Refulgence. Similarly, in the thrid prayer, Death represents Loss, temporality, suffering, desease and old age, while Immortality, though having a very wide reference, is essentially about Freedom, Eternity, Joy, Fullness and Vigour.

Now, it is clear from this prayer that in the perception of the ancients the human condition was not at all propitous. It was riddled with imperfections to which sorrow and suffering were endemic. It is equally important to note that they passionately desired to move out of this situation and transform the human condition in the light of their vision of perfection. Man has never took it lying down as it were. He desired to conquer the imperfection with his scientific and spiritual knowledge of reality. So, both, his perception and his aspiration with regard to his condition are ingredients in the human conditions. This is characteristic of the human being. He is not content with the 'given'. He must act to transform himself and his environment to find his perfections in the being of what IS, in the light of enlightenment and in the power of Immortality. Again it is important to note that in a hermeneutical understanding of these hyms "human perfection and happiness are always viewed from an integrated perspective, which embraces both material and spiritual values in one indivisible and harmonious unity" (R. Panikkar, *The Vedic Experience*, p. 296). However, this journey from Darkness to Light is not smooth. There is an abyss between man's perception of his human condition and his aspiration to transform it. In a phenomenological perspective this abyss is the darkness of a primeval FEAR.

In all the three elements in the perception of the human condition, namely the IS NOT, the Darkness and Death, the primary emotion that arises is fear. Fear then becomes the central operational force in conditioning subsequent existence. There are all kinds of fear depending upon the nature of the objects which immediately cause them. Fear is congenital. Religion has often invoked the fear of God to strengthen moral behaviour in men, and the faith in the goodness of God to overcome his fear of nature and of his fellow men. Then there is the fear of the great unknown, of what may happen tomorrow. Then there is also the fear of the past. In the schema of the human condition sketched in the prayers, we can clearly spot the following incipient strands of fear. 'Is Not' in symbolic of the fear of emptiness both in its material and spiritual connotations. The consciousness of 'emptiness' produces the dread of not-having, not-possessing the resources of survival, of defence, of flourish, of pleasure and fulfilment, and above all, spiritually, of not being able to identify oneself with anything substantial. Thus Is Not in its existential resolution is essentially the fear of "non-being". Similarly Darkness provokes the fear of the unperceived danger of evil. It arouses the fear of loosing the energy associated with the sun, of sinking into the dissipating depression of loneliness. It is a fear of loosing colourful, joyful brilliance of perceptible, tangible qualities of life. Again these are the existential attributes of becoming a no-thing, and consequently a source of generating the fear of non-being. Lastly, the third element of Death clearly produces the fear of impermanence, of insignificance and meaninglessness or existence. Spiritually it is a feeling of alienation from being. It signifies decay of the power of 'becoming', and therefore provokes the fear of the World. Indeed Death is most definitively the symbol of nothingness or non-being.

In this way we can see that the fear of non-being is at the centre of human existence. It is the alienated essence of the human condition perceived as Is Not, Darkness and Death. In the existential situation it becomes the driving force behind concrete achievements. Even the quest of truth and Immortality are often quite visibly a way of hiding this fear. But what is this fear in itself? In asking this question we are inviting the enquirer to hold to consciousness, at the highest level of phenomenological reflection, the essence we have identified, i.e. 'non-being', without the objects which the feeling of fear may be intending. Thus denying it any objectivity, any reference to context and any intentionality, one apprehends the primal fear in the absolute. In this reductive exercise one discovers that left by itself the Fear begins to melt away. It exists only in a relational thought of oneself in a situation of non-being. For example, walking on a street in Bangalore if I suddenly encounter a Bengal tiger, in the initial moments there is no fear. It comes in on at once at the thought "it might attack". And the fear arises because we have already placed ourselves in the permanent situation of the human condition considered, as demonstrated earlier, in its aspect of non-being. So the all important question arises if our initial placement of ourselves under the permanent threat of non-being in the human condition, is a correct view of reality. And to be able to answer this question, it is obvious that we need the correct view of the human self itself—the self which is believed to be placed thus and so in its own perception. For this reason the enquiry into the nature of the self has been central to philosophy in India, and to spiritual phenomenology in particular.

Reflection on the contemporary condition reveals that the all-pervading influence of fear is great in conditioning existence. Instead of trying to find ways of conquering it, man has desparately searched for "substitutes"—which is a mechanism of suppression of fear and the creation of an illusion of fulfilment. Let us see how the story of the substitution process unfolds itself in actual existence.

A recognition of the universal presence of Fear and the dread of it is sufficiently evidenced in many of the hymns in the *Atharva Veda*: (Vi. 40)

1. Breathe on us fearlessness, Heaven and Earth!
   by the strength of the Omnipresent Soma
   by the light of the Omniscient Savitre
   may we be free of fear!
2. From the North and the South, the East and the West
   let the light of god Savitre
   direct on this land
   sustenance, welfare and ease
   May the power of God Indra grant us freedom from foes
   removing all fear deflecting all.

Note: These gods or Gods are conceived in the earliest *Rig Veda* as aspects of the manifest powers of an all-inclusive "One Divine Reality" called *"Brahman"*. This concept of the One has been the source of most subsequent philosophy in India, including the philosophy of the ways of removing the core fear. The reference to its divinity is instructive. The reality is not mere 'matter' of modern science but a unity of aspects of the material, the living and the spiritual, thus providing a rational basis for man's aspiration to transform the human condition.

Today the collective acceptance of violence as a legitimate means of resolving conflcit, together with an aggressive individualism and consumerism, have become settled social features of our culture. The individualism of the priority of self-interest that is invoked is nothing but a desparate self-assertion of an egoistic man who is afraid of the world and sees others as snatchers of their individual lot, rather than as partners in the common enterprise of 'self-realization' of the Humanity. Fear is always alienating, setting up the individual in competition with the community. Indeed aggressive competition with the 'other', at all levels from the individual to the national, has become the key to success in a free-market economy. But it only adds the fear of being trampled over in the race for "more". Consumerism is the natural psychological outcome of this fear. Owning, possessing and consuming more and more seems to have evolved as the substitute mechanism for repression of fear. The craving for more cannot be explained away as simply a normal desire for the satisfaction of the material needs of survival and the creative enjoyment of life. There is certainly a touch of the 'neurotic' there.

We tend to think that 'possessing' will end the feeling of alienation, and the feeling of insecurity caused by it. But the substitutes succeed only in increasing the fear of being left on one own. Loneliness and depression are the immediate spin-offs from the success of such individualism. And in reaction to these, people are often driven to suicide and other acts of social violence. The existential manifestations of the fear of non-being are only too common across cultures.

The desire for possessing power is natural to the insecure man. Possessions in the form of wealth, fame and knowledge, all in their own ways produce a feeling of power over others and over the human situation generally. Even artistic achievement gives that feeling *via* establishing one's authority and of course often receiving disproportionately huge amounts of money. There will be very few people today who pursue the arts for the love of the goods internal to those activities, namely for the love of humanity, truth and beauty. The desire for power is obviously connected with the feeling of insecurity whose roots are in the primordial Fear which we have located in our perception of the human condition.

Further, there is another existential crisis located right in the heart of the individual. Torn between ambition and duty we seem to grow up with a huge conflict within our hearts. On the one hand, the values of a capitalistic society tell us to be ambitious, competitive, achievers, ready to tread on others if need be there, on the other, we are constantly fed with the values of a religious ethics which tells us that as children of God, the whole mankind is one family, and we should be Kind, giving and forgiving to others. But when we go out into the world we feel compelled to live with a ruthless pragmatism. Obviously personal ambition and caring for others do not go together. And unfortunately, having evolved from animals man has inherited the jungle fears, which, instinctively, he tries to allay with recourse to violence. Thus the so called civilized man has created vast amounts of built-in violence in the structures of social organizations. Given such condition of the contemporary life, we can see that our perception of the human condition, and the ensuing primordial fear has not only not changed but has found new existential substitutes in more persuasive and globalised forms of life. One is perhaps a reminded that 'the point however', of these insights 'is to change' the world.

The misery of the conditioned existence cannot be removed without eliminating the primordial fear completely. For this, as indicated earlier, the human condition itself needs to be transformed. If the human condition were an objective feature of reality we would not be able to do anything about it. But since fortunately it exists only in the perception of the soul, which is a state of consciousness, we can certainly do something about it. As noted earlier, in the wisdom of the sages, the way of self-knowledge is the right way to it. In this regard a phenomenological approach obviously has an edge over other analytical approaches. Here we are dealing with the reality of states of consciousness. And a concept of the reality is never the thing itself. Moreover, mere conceptual analysis, to echo Passmore, like a constant whetting of the knife when nothing is meant to cut with it, is ever engaged in sharpening its tools without explaining how the gap between the thing and its concept is to be bridged.

The Way of Self-Knowledge

Surely a complete self-knowledge must impart the understanding of what it means to be an embodied self, i.e. a human being, at all the levels of human existence, namely, the material, biological, the mental and the spiritual. Further since human life exists in relationship, self-knowledge must also involve understanding oneself-in-relationship to entities both of the impersonal and personal nature. The peculiarity of the human being is that he exists at all these levels simultaneously. He is never a mere body, mind or spirit separately, as long as he is alive. Then on each of these levels he seems to be connected with larger wholes of appropriate types. Thus physically he is made of the elements of his natural environment, and a constant exchange of energy with it must be assured for survival. He is literally a part of the whole of nature considered as an interconnected self-sustaining living system. Mentally too the individual self is not a solipsistic substance. His mind is a sub-system within the larger whole of the collective mind of humanity. This is clear from the fact that he would not even come to possess the conceptual unity of a human mind at all without being constantly placed in a learning situation of a communicative interaction with others. And spiritually there is no doubt that the biological entity 'man' as a *being* is constituted within an integrated spiritual reality of being-consciousness. This can be demonstrated as follows: The spirituality of man is generally characterized in terms of his power of transcendence. We notice a constant fulfilment of this power in the world, first, in each act of self-consciousness in which the given empirical self is surpassed and objectified in a non-cognitive awareness, and simultaneously the transcendental self is apprehended as pure being-consciousness, unlocated and timeless. Next, the power of transcendence is manifest in human creativity where consciousness breaks away from the conditioned existence into the pure spontaneity of freedom. The self is an ill-encompassing phenomenon of the individualization of existence. And self-knowledge should reveal both its empirical and transcendental dimensions in the entire range of its constitution.

From this brief reflection upon the nature of the embodied self, the picture that emerges is that the self cannot be analysed away reductively into body, mind and spirit and then the three put together 'externally', to constitute a human being. Its uniqueness lies in its indivisible inclusivity comprising of all the known aspects of reality, as though God had made man in his own image. At the same time it is equally clear that no man is an Island to himself or in himself. Because he is ontologically interconnected and interdependent within the whole of existence, his 'self' represents an open system perhaps like the universe itself. So the role of human perception in organizing and presenting the human situation, and subsequently in apprehending the human condition, must be crucial.

The moral and psychological fall out of this realization is immense. It shatters his loneliness, destroys his alienation from being and his desparate individualism to cope with them. By reconnecting him with all humanity and nature, it restores his human dignity and implants in him a sense of belonging to the whole. The knowledge that he is an inseparable part of the world teaches him that "you are the world". Naturally then it produces an extraordinary sense of responsibility for the whole. It gives him a sense of deep respect for all life and humanity. And above all, the sense of belonging to the whole is the ending of that fear whose existential mutations, as we have seen, weave together this ugly culture of selfishness. Indeed it is freedom from fear of non-being.

All the same, the self-knowledge that we have arrived at so far is merely intellectual. Such understanding, though not without significance, yet fails to make a radical transformative impact upon the psychic roots of existence. How can the human primordial fear be totally annihilated? Since it is individual centred, and arises in the individual's perception of the human condition, it is only logical to infer that the eleminative action has to be upon the individual and within his personal consciousness. This fact underlines the role of social institutions in creating a favourable climate in a free and just society, for the eliminative exercises to be conducted. Further it is also clear that the desired action has to transform the individual's perception of the human condition and his own relation to it. Since the human condition is essentially a perceived phenomenon, both these factors, namely his perception and his emotional relation to the human condition, are within the constitution of the individual self.

It follows, therefore, that whatever the eliminative action be, it has to be on the self and by one's own self, and in that sense it would be a spiritual action.

To begin with, we have to realize that we are deeply conditioned into the belief that a human being has a permanent enduring self, in the form of a unique spiritual substance or a soul, one for each individual. This belief is encouraged by the fact that the "I" represents a unitary centre of consciousness, and memories arising in the present connect the ownership of a personal past with the present I-consciousness. Thus we take it for granted that inwardly we remain one and the same entity throughout our constantly changing biography. But when we look inwards we are horrified to discover that we encounter only shifting states of consciousness. And when we try to go behind the scenes, as it were, and locate the transcendental "I", we encounter an even more horrifying scenario—a vast 'emptiness', an awareness without the centre of the individual ego. And then the conceptual mind moves in swiftly to identify the unrecognizable, the unknowable, as an object of knowledge. Consciousness then gives it a name, a symbol, an image. This naming divides consciousness which in itself is 'whole', into the subject and the object. Thus it is the operation of thought upon the given undivided phenomenon of being-consciousness, that creates the individual self and simultaneously a world for it to engage in. We need to go deeper, in a phenomenological mode of enquiry, into ourselves and perceive directly the moment in which the individual self-consciousness appears like a wave in the ocean of existence. We must catch ourselves in apperceptions in the moment of the original encounter with the human condition, in relation to an individual ego. Only then we can understand the whole truth about the self and the truth about the origin of Fear. It is clear from this that the action that would lead him to that understanding will have to be of the nature of direct, non-linguistic and non-interpretative awareness. In our times there is a compelling account of this kind of self-perception in the spiritual philosophy of J. Krishnamurti. Let us see how he conducts his exploration.

Krishnamurti maintains that the moment of the divisive action of thought separating the subject from the object, can be accessed directly in what he calls "choiceless awareness". Briefly, it is an awareness of the action of the thought-process in an attentiveness which does not indulge in the contents of the thought. That is, it does not disturb the intentionality of the thought. Further it is a way of attending to the whole field of thought, including its emotional surrounding, without encouraging or discouraging the motivational force that it carries. This attentive consciousness is completely alert, passive and undivided. It is simply aware of 'what is', moving spontaneously over the whole field of thought. Generally we do not realize that we have this capacity to summon pure attention and 'observe without the observer' directing the observation. We do not realize that attention is different from thought, though both are movements in one infinity of consciousness. If we can observe the "what is" in this undivided choiceless awareness, we will see that we do not rush to interpret the human condition in the way we originally did it. In Krishnamurti's meditation one does not immediately and delibrately direct the mind upon the essence of whatever is to be known. The essence may not be conceptually determinable. It may be a disclosure of some timeless reality. Obviously the essence is something to be arrived at through a successful enquiry.

One begins with an *unfocused* awareness, without concentrating on anything, with total attention turned upon the operational self as it is actually implicated in day-to-day life. Then, in choiceless awareness of the engagement of thought, operating within the dualistic framework, consciousness begins to wage through the interpretative and the connative aspects of its present state. And then, again, putting aside all the urges to 'commit' oneself to the thought-contents, i.e. to say inwardly the Cartesian 'yes' or 'no' to judge it, one arrives at the point of the very origin of thought itself. At this point one does not encounter a thinker as a separate entity, giving rise to the thought *ab initio.* On the contrary one finds that when consciousness curls upon itself, the I- consciousness arises as an aspect of the thought under which the thought is considered 'owned' by a thinker. This knowledge is a direct perception of *how* the world of thought is constituted at its very origin, and so of how it is related to the timeless. This knowledge itself being 'outside' thought cannot be put into words. It is a knowing-in-being, a knowing without the knower. "Those who actually know it say they cannot conceive it." (*Kenopnishad*)

Thus the "self" stands exposed. Its secret is revealed. The being of the individual self has no separate ontological reality. This is real self-knowledge by acquaintance with the point of origin of the I-consciousness. The illusion of separateness from the life-world has completely ended. One is now free to look at the human condition in clear light. One can imagine the total impact of this self-realization. When there is no ontological gap between the individual self and the Reality, then where is the room for the primordial Fear! It is freedom from fear of non-being into the Light of Truth. One has already moved into the IS of the prayer, and into the Immortality of a moment-to-moment Creativity, of a constantly dying and incarnating self. Finally, I wish to end my reflections with a futuristic note on the human condition. It is common knowledge that with the advent of the genetic science and the advancements in the computer science, a completely new possibility has emerged for mankind. They may remove fear altogether. They may alter the brain in such a way that it may become insensitive to the spiritual dimensions of consciousness that we have considered, especially the 'lacks' we perceive in the human condition. They may throw away, as it were, the baby with the bath water, though in other ways the biological 'man' may become a super species. It is possible that man may conquer disease, old age and even death. But will it be worth it; if mankind looses that aesthetic feeling for creativity, that longing for a spiritual completeness, which provides for the greatest adventure in living? Devoid of the aesthetic dimensions of existence, the very essence of humanity, will he not turn into simply super automata? We sincerely hope that it will never happen. What is important, however, is to realize that it is all up to us now. The primordial human condition may be one of insufficiency, but it is neither unresourceful nor of eternal bondage to nature.

I have tried to say how the perception of the *human condition conditions existence*. But there are also the intimations of the Truth and the Light and the Immortality in the same existence. It is up to us to pick on this or that side of the horn. If, however, it is asked what good is it to mankind in general, if one Buddha, one Christ, one Gandhi and so on have confronted the FEAR and eliminated it from their lives, we have only to remember what massive transformations of the human psyche they have affected, and what humanity may have been without those effects.

6

KRISHNAMURTI'S CONCEPTION OF HOLISTIC EDUCATION

In modern times most thinkers on education have advocated an ideal of holistic education. Even in ancient India, when unfortunately education was not available to all, the *Gurukulas* seem to have practised an inclusive concept of education. Apart from covering all branches of knowledge known in those days, the inmates were required to live together and participate in all the work of the school including such mundane things as cooking and cleaning. In this process they imbibed the values of 'sharing and caring' which are so essential for the growth of a moral outlook towards life and the sacred nature of 'learning'. In modern western educational philosophy, since the 17th century onwards, there has been a considerable concern for a holistic pattern of education, trying to cover physical training including sports, scientific and humanistic training including performative arts and spiritual training including religion and ethics. The slogan is, as recently coveted by R.S. Peters, that education must be of "the whole man".

In modern India we have been trying, perhaps half-heartedly, to emulate this conception with almost a total disaster and a total loss of our ancient insights as well in this matter. So, it seems to me that we have to raise the question concerning what constitutes holistic education afresh. Could, in particular, separate instruction in individual disciplines, even if varied enough, add up to an education of 'the whole man'? I am going to suggest that it does not. The traditional approaches fail to individuate the 'whole' concerned simply because they fail to appreciate the principle of unity behind it. In this regard the Socratic insight shared by

Krishnamurti maintains that 'the learning of many things does not make one wise', implying that wisdom is something of a holistic quality of education, which is not contained in learning many subjects accumulatively. It also shows that the goal of education of the whole man is to enable a person to live a fruitful and fulfilling life, sensitive to the fact of the 'unity and integrity' of a human being considered as a unitary centre of consciousness. To justify the use of the term 'holistic' for the educational process, it must produce, firstly, an integrated understanding of knowledge, and secondly, an integrated view of its significance for the individual's life considered as a whole. Similarly, to justify the talk of educating the whole man we must clearly identify the characteristic unity of human life, both in its temporal extension and in its indivisible personal consciousness. The term 'holistic' is qualitative and not a quantitative concept; the whole is not simply the sum of its parts but signifies a quality not present in any of its parts taken singly or in a compound.

The importance of the ideal of holistic education cannot be overemphasised, especially in the present age, when pressures of specialisation has put both, education and the educated, in a state of total fragmentation. Though in the age of scientific excellence, the need of specialisation cannot be denied, one has to find a way of how to accommodate it without sacrificing the concern for educating the 'whole man'. Education in the present age, in consonance with the ethos of the culture of individualism and consumerism, has become simply an exercise in acquiring useful skills and information to enable one to do specific jobs and solve specialised problems of overt nature. In this it leaves out the "wisdom" which is necessary for understanding and solving personal psychological problems arising in day-do-day human relationship. It leaves out that vast area of conduct in which cultural meanings are stated and socially contested. In this purely utilitarian perspective, education is simply a means to attaining certain profitable ends. But surely, in an important sense education is also an end in itself, since the growth of knowledge and understanding it bestows, is constitutive of our humanity. The conversion of a mere biological entity 'man' into a human being through education has been traditionally called his rebirth and the educated man is called "twice-born".

I think it will be generally agreed that the immediate goal of education is creation, advancement and transmission of knowledge, and further, in this process to enable the individual to attain a full flowering of his intelligence as a social, intellectual and spiritual being. But true knowledge must be distinguished from mere information, even true information, and techniques of doing things. Of course, having knowledge is being able to apply it, but being able to apply a piece of information does not by itself amount to 'having knowledge'. So the mechanism and the method by which a belief is converted into knowledge is of utmost importantce. In this process the learner acquires the ability to make a creative use of knowledge. Moreover, since knowledge is both for the use of human beings and constitutive of human beings, it is important that the user knows who or what he is and what are his wider goals in life *as a human being.* In other words he appreciates the significance of knowledge in human life *per se.* He realises that he is not simply using his knowledge mechanically, nor on the dictates of some authority for fear or greed. Education must impart this human dignity and integrity to the educated man.

This is possible only if the educated man knows himself and understands how he is constituted by his beliefs in his attitudes, intentions and emotions. So, if education is to accomplish the goal of educating the whole man, knowledge must be supervised by self-knowledge. Indeed knowledge without self-knowledge is blind and is more likely to bring chaos than order in social life. In our times J. Krishnamurti is the best known exponent of the view which puts self-knowing at the centre of education. Let us see how he unfolds his ideas.

Traditionally self-knowledge has always been central to Indian spiritual discourses. There, except for the Buddha, the self has been considered as an individual spiritual substance, separable at death, and permanent throughout the individual's life. But this conception of the self relegates self-knowledge to the domain of the occult. Krishnamurti rejects this notion. Nor is he interested in the metaphysical notion of the self which the followers of the Buddha developed. Rather, his focus in this matter lies upon understanding the operational nature of the self. Unlike the philosopher he does not produce a theory of the self, and turns his attention to the actual manifestations of the self in daily life. In his insightful hands the whole discourse receives a completely new meaning, away from the tradition. Krishnamurti recognises that the self is present in each and every act of consciousness we engage in. The self is thus *an aspect of an act* under which the act is considered 'owned' by an agent. The owner, the subject or the experiencer is then thought to be an entity separate from the act. But Krishnamurti considered in some detail, in which we need not enter here, that the thinker is not separate from the thought, the experiencer is not separate from the experience and so on. There is no ontological gap between the self and the states of consciousness it inhabits. In this perspective, therefore, self-knowledge is not a matter of introspective psychology; it becomes a matter of understanding the phenomenological contents of experience in the operational "ways of the self" in all its movements. Moreover, not being an abstract intellectual discourse, it is available to everyone in the very act of knowing the world in ordinary cognitive achievements. In particular, it is a matter of discovering the motivational structures of conscious acts of all kinds that we engage in. Thus self-knowledge, moving along with knowledge amounts to a complete existential understanding of life itself, in all its physical mental and spiritual manifestations.

It seems to me obvious that knowledge without self-knowledge is blind to the value and significance of knowledge for life considered as a whole. Without self-knowledge not only we cannot attain an integrated view of knowledge, we cannot even know what purpose it is to serve and therefore what direction it ought to take. In short, without self-knowledge we will be unable to make a creative use of knowledge. By self-knowledge however (it should be clear from what I have already said about the self) I do not mean the occult perception of some glorious spiritual substance within. What I mean is the understanding of what it means to be a human being. Education must impart this understanding and enable us to put specialised knowledge in its proper place in the total scheme of values. First, we must realise that the human being exists at three different levels simultaneously—the biological, the mental and the spiritual. This is the peculiarity of man. At no level of his existence, however, he is an absolutely separate individual in an ontological sense. Physically he is made of the elements of his natural environment and a constant exchange of energy with the elements must be assured. He is literally a part of the whole of nature considered as an interconnected self-sustaining system. Mentally too he is not a Cartesian solipsistic substance. His mind is a sub-system within the larger whole of the social mind and eventually the collective mind of the humanity. This is shown by the fact that indeed he will not come to possess a human mind in the first place if he were not constantly in a learning situation of communicative interaction with other minds for whom the same is true, thus signifying a constant run of mentality from the beginning of animal life. Each individual is, therefore, responsible for the whole within which he is inseparably constituted. Any radical change in him will naturally mark a change in the whole. Since he is an integral part of the whole, in a sense the individual and the world are not dualistically opposed to each other. An spiritually, there is no doubt that the individual is like a wave in the ocean of existence. This is shown by the fact that neither his creativity nor his transcendence of the 'given' are realisations of his individually located will. His spiritual consciousness is something that happens to him rather than something produced by his specific will. Only his ego separates him from the rest. But even if his ego is rightly perceived his act of constant self-transcendence will be reminding him that he necessarily belonged to the whole. Unfortunately our education in its analytical accretions emphasises the relative separateness of things and not their interconnectedness or the inter-dependence. Our culture of materialism does the same. Your success is accredited as your individual achievement, whereas in fact it is a success of humanity. Unfortunately our educational system today, under the pressure of specialisation, does not only not include self-knowledge, it is mostly becoming 'informational'. But acquisition of knowledge proper is surely something more than gathering information. When I read a book or attend a lecture and remember the contents, I am not necessarily acquiring knowledge. At the most I am acquiring beliefs which if hopefully true may prove useful in certain circumstances. Knowledge is something which *belongs* to the individual. It is assimilated in his total conceptual repertoire in such a way that enables him to make an original use of it. It happens when the truths embedded in the acquired piece of information are discovered by the learner himself. The act of discovering a truth by oneself has the effect of transforming the attitude of the individual towards all those facts that are significantly related to the discovery. For example, if a person discovers that some 'harm' done to him was unintentional and done in ignorance of the facts, his bitterness towards the wrong-doer is bound to melt away. In theoretical situations too the discovery of a truth is bound to bring about a reorganisation of a whole scheme of truths relevant to the former. Here it will be retorted that one cannot and need not discover all the truths by oneself. That is so, but for information to translate into knowledge the truths in question must be rediscovered by the agent. For this there has to be restructuring of the learning situation. Apart from the experimental situations there has to be dialogical and interactive situations. Only then it will add to his creative potential and transform his outlook. It is the same with self-knowledge. If I knew who or what I am at all the levels of my existence, that is, if I knew that I am not an Island to myself, then my feelings and relationship with everything around me is bound to change. The fact of interconnectedness and inter-dependence at all levels of my being is bound to transform my outlook towards the whole. A complete spiritually informed self-knowledge will end our xenophobia and violence upon nature. Then there will be compassion, and a sense of responsibility for the whole will be natural to this enlightened human being.

The Challenge of Modernity

In order to understand the challenge in question, we first have to be impressed by the nature and the extent of change in the character of modern societies. The following features seem to me to be directly relevant to the project of rethinking about education. Modern societies have considerably distanced themselves from religion in the sense that basic social institutions are no longer organised around religious beliefs, whereas in the past it was just the opposite. So modernity requires a new way of relating human values to the life of the society. A modern society is a legal polity, embracing some form of democracy. So culture must create new social institutions to provide the individual with relevant opportunities for responsible participation in the social life. Further, to a large extent, cultural dissemination took place through the institution of the family. But the family's scope and meaning has radically changed. So new kinds of associations, such as clubs and specific interest-catering centres have to evolve. Again, the community can no longer exercise direct cultural control over the individual. Modern individualism censors and resists that kind of control. Here again much needs to be done. Since one role of culture is to enable the individual to achieve a private ordering of personal meanings.

The way of life of a modern (industrial) society is under constant pressure to make adjustments, to adopt new ways of doing things. This suggests an end of the era of "tradition". New discoveries in science and technology are constantly influencing the human perspective upon life, and forcing man to redefine his relationship with man, nature as well as the machine. The public and private goals, ends and purposes are under constant revision. In the past social groups could exist in their splendid isolations. They were under no pressure to change. And in due course of time their cultures lost the spirit of the quest. Ritual replaced the reason for the existence of their beliefs and practices. In this regard modernity has done them good service. For, a lively culture must be perpetually disturbed, discontented. Modernity has brought this discontent to the doorsteps of all of us. Now societies are unconsciously constantly changing. But that is a change under pressure and compulsion; it is governed by the blind logic of growth, of the cry of 'me' and 'more'. And compulsion is never creative. So we need individuals who are free from such compulsions, who possess freedom of consciousness—not just social freedom. Such individuals have made an inner rebellion against authority—authority in matters of truth, in morals and values. Such freedom is necessary for creativity. So the fundamental challenge of modernity is this: How to enable ourselves and our children to grow up to live our lives quest fully? How to develop the holistic sensibility of culture that I have sketched? How to regain the respect for nature and life (which, ironically, was so characteristic of the tribal outlook)? How to maintain the unity and sanctity of life without retracting from the analytical knowledge of modern science, and without returning to the nature of the Romantics, or to the spirituality of the forest? And above all, how to introduce the quality of love and compassion in our social relationship?

I am going to suggest that it is education which can bring about the right kind of transformation within the individual to enable him to meet the challenge in question. But it has to be an education which is at once directed upon both the 'subject' and the 'object'—an education in which 'knowing' and 'self-knowing' move together. Unfortunately this is not happening. We have divided life in many segments : public and private, personal and professional, youth and old age and so on. The morning is separated from the evening in a way that we are unable to experience the beauty of the day as a whole. In the pursuit of knowledge relevant to 'success' in each separate segment, man is becoming more and more specialised but less and less integrated. Psychologically and spiritually we are becoming very very shallow and superficial; because knowledge which is always limited, fragmentary, is replacing wisdom which is always holistic.

Educating the 'Whole' Child

In the contemporary world the totalistic role of schools cannot be overemphasised. The right education requires creating right kind of schools which are more than centres of formal instruction. This would no doubt require a great deal of institutional and material support. Briefly, by the right kind of school I mean the following. It is not merely a place where ideologically selective 'information' is deposited in the heads of the children. Rather it is a place which has the character of "a community of inquiry". In addition, it is a place where the child has all the facilities to nurture his body as well as his specific talents and intersts, without being subjected to harsh discipline and punishment. In such a school the teacher is not seen as an embodiment of 'authority' in matters of truth and value. This is not to say that he does not present to the pupil the facts and figures of formal education as true and valuable. There will always be that kind of work to be done. But the child is not made to feel that the matter is closed for the teacher says so. Instead the teacher will try to establish a 'dialogical' relationship with the pupil and encourage the same between them. This can be achieved in a class room situation by reading and discussing a narrative with the spirit of inquiry, and outside the class, by sharing in a form of life in the spirit of freindship. The informational content of formal education, then, will fall in its right place for the over all growth of his personality. In a dialogical relationship the teacher is also essentially an inquirer, and the children get the feeling of discovering the facts and values for themselves, rather than simply receiving them from the teacher. And that is not all. The teacher must enable the child to discover where his real interest lies, and the child should be helped to pursue it. Discipline too should be a matter of discovering the behaviour necessary to the learning process. Children should learn and do things for the love of learning, rather than be forced to learn, or motivated to learn, for some sort of reward external to learning. Moreover, it is important to realise, that right education is not limited only to schools. Indeed to be living a human life is to be located in an educational situation all the time. One has to learn without being taught. This will happen naturally to those who have been to the right kind of schools others have to make the required orientation on their own. Such learning is learning about life, and about the significance of formal education for life considered as a whole—the life that includes death. This amounts to self-knowing : discovering oneself-in-relationship. This notion of self-knowledge involves understanding why we live the way we do—struggling to satisfy our greed and ambitions for power, wealth and status, or, alternatively, resigned to fate or 'what will be will be'. It is this understanding which brings the transformation within the individual, which, as we have seen, is essential to meet the challenge of modernity. For, as it is well noted, it is the truth that frees you—freedom from the evil and the ugly. In truth the negation of the ugly within ourselves make us beautiful as persons. And the negation of the evil of greed and ambition makes us caring and compassionate. This kind of self-knowing, involving 'inner freedom' is important for all if culture is to improve the quality of human life holistically; for such freedom is the fountain of creativity.

Furthermore, perhaps the most significant deliverance of this kind of self-knowledge is, that through it, one is able to experience (not just intellectually accept) the reality of the interconnectedness of all things. Such experience is enlightenment, which discloses to us our real (spiritual) needs as human beings, and defines the role of knowledge in fulfilling those needs. Such enlightenment is also the sole source of the sense of responsibility so essential to cultural consciousness.

We can now draw a clearer picture of the right kind of education that I have suggested. Education is of the 'whole' man: this can be achieved only if we stop teaching the child that success in one of the arts or the sciences is the sole aim of life.

The key concepts of educational process are 'critical', 'dialogical', 'innovative' and 'observational'.

Learning must also be simultaneously a case of self-knowing; the latter is not a matter of formal education. Education is to awaken the desire for learning for the love of life, and not merely to be able to do a job.

Education should make us appreciate the inter-dependence of all things: The realisation that as an individual person one is internally connected with others within a scheme of nature, is the source of respect for others and the basis for moral relationship. It is also the source of respect for nature, and the basis of the 'love of life'. The idea of interconnectedness should not be misunderstood. It does not mean that the individual is first a complete separate entity, and then, externally, *dependent* upon others. We are not teaching that you are at the mercy of others or of the society, for that matter. Rather the recognition of interconnectedness gives you a sense of *belonging* to the 'whole'. It is this feeling of belonging that provides the ground for responsibility. The sense of responsibility is at the centre of an integrated development of human personality.

A questful approach to life leads to a creative engagement with life, and that is surely the right way to live.

The competitive spirit should be eliminated and replaced with the cooperative spirit. It is a myth that competition is necessary for personal progress. In the latter case each one does his best for the love of excellence. If this sounds too unrealistic in the present age, let us remember that even in a non-team game a good player's mind-set is not competitive. The player concentrates on his own game doing his very best, because that is the best way to play. If he is distracted by the thought 'I must do better *than him*' he will be playing with divided attention and will be unable to summon his total energy to the task. Consequently he is more likely to lose. When one takes a 'competitive examination', one's own psychology cannot be that one is competing with other candidates, whom he does not even know. Competition as such is the point of view of the selection committee.

The produce of such education will be a self-knowing, integrated true individual, who will always be a challenge to the destructive forces of modernity. He will be the bearer of the true spirit and sensibility of the culture of mankind irrespective of his geographical and historical location. One who is able to produce the good of human life is able to carry others along with him, for *that* good is good for everyone.

The stress should be on participatory inquiry into issues which matter to the children themselves. And the teacher should be able to appreciate the child's point of view. They should be encouraged to observed their natural and social environment, and relate their class room knowledge to real life, in a personally meaningful way. Most importantly children should be helped to find reasons for their personal beliefs, and helped to distinguish the objective and universal, from the purely subjective and individual. The idea is to develop concept-formation, rational thought, responsibility and self-knowledge using material which is factually informative, contemporary and culturally relevant. Such education helps the child to think for himself, providing space for his mind to grow in a way so that he is not anchored to belief, to traditions, and not oppressed by fear; and therefore he is free and creative.

We must begin, then, the educational-revolution-for-culture by creating the right kind of schools and making them available to all children. Since so much depends upon the right kind of teacher, he should be made to feel secure, both economically and psychologically. The school environment should make him feel at home, cared for, without financial worries. We have to remember that Education is at once both, an ingredient in an enlightened culture and the essential instrument for a constant advancement of culture.[1]

Moral and Value Education

In the present educational circles there is a great deal of talk of value education, including moral, social and aesthetic values. But value education is surely a practical matter which our schools and colleges are least equipped to deal with. Moral education, for example, is not a matter of learning a set of principles, 'commandments' or a set of virtues and then being told to go and practise them in real life. Life being what it is, constantly places us in ever-new situations. Morality being an aspect of life-in-relationship in relevant to each and every situation. So even if we had a hand book of moral principles, we would not know how to apply them in real life. Moreover, morality refers to human freedom. We cannot live our moral life on the authority of another person. But the morality of all the holy books and the wisdom and prohibitions of the social traditions are all derived from some or other authority. A moral choice involves the whole being of a person. It engages his total sensibility. So the question for moral education is not what principles a child should be taught, but what kind of education in general will make him morally capable. Krishnamurti goes to the heart of the problem:

> "If our behaviour is direced by the environment in which we live, controlled and shaped by it, then it is mechanical and heavily conditioned. And if our behaviour is the outcome of our own conditioned response, is it moral? If our action is based on fear and reward, is it righteous? If you behave rightly according to some ideological concept or principle, can that action be regarded as virtuous? So we must begin to find out how deeply we have discarded the morality of authority, imitation, conformity and obedience."[2]

Krishnamurti's message is abundantly clear. Freedom from 'authority, imitation, conformity and obedience' is the essence of moral education. If the goal of moral education is to enable the children to become 'morally-capable', then there total development has to take place in the cradle of holistic education which we have sketched. As it is our whole educational system is based on the values of personal success operated by the mechanism of reward and punishment. Indeed it is a perfect embodiment of the morality of authority, imitation, conformity and obedience all of which has to be discarded. We have seen that holistic education centred around self-knowledge is the way to the required freedom from the conditioned cultural background. This self-knowing freedom is the source of that sense of responsibility for the whole, which is so central to morality. Equipped with this sense of responsibility and the compassion which goes with it, the individual does not need any specific moral principles to live his life. Virtue is natural to this individual, for he has imbibed the ethics of 'caring and sharing' in all aspects of life, throughout his educational development. For him moral education is not a separate kind of education; it is an integral part of life. The above remarks about moral education are equally valid for value education generally. Value education is not a matter of theoretical instruction. The child should be allowed to develop his own sense of values. Truth, goodness and beauty have intrinsic value in all their manifestations. The child has to be led into a total development of his sensibility, his sense of discrimination and evaluation, or what Krishnamurti calls *"the full flowering of humanity"*. This is possible when education is completely free from indoctrination and authority. In the present climate there is deep split in value education. On the one hand we are indoctrinated into universal human values—freedom, equality, justice and so on—and on the other, in actual life, both individually and collectively, we are encouraged into sectarian values of competition, domination and putting self-interest above all other things. As a result the child grows up with a conflict in his very psyche. We cannot then expect him to manifest social harmony in his adult life. When our individual development is inherently neurotic, we cannot expect to create a society which is based in universal human values. As a result all our social institutions, including the educational, are stepped in cruelty and selfishness. To be able to transcend this situation education must allow that children to grow in complete freedom from conformity and obedience to authority. The learning process must engage them in 'enquiry', 'observation' and 'understanding' rather than a mechanical learning impelled by the motive of reward and fear. As we have seen, the holistic education sensitive to self-knowledge does engage them in this way. In the atmosphere of freedom, children engage in learning for the love of life, without the motive of profit. To teach them to work for the love of doing things is to give them the best form of value education.

NOTES

1. In writing this chapter I am repeatedly guided by the ideas of J. Krishnamurti. See his : *This Matter of Culture* and *Letters to the Schools* (Krishnamurti Foundation, India).
2. *The Second Penguine Krishnamurti Reader*, ed. Mary Lutyens, p. 210.

7

SECULARISM

The essence of Secularism is this: That political power should not give to any particular, religious group a privileged access to the nations resources. These resources include power, wealth and intellect. From this it follows that, in India, the majority group of Hindus will not have special access to education or employment or trade and commerce. And this much is enshrined in the Constitution of India. The point is that secularism in politics looked at in this way is a function of the full and fair play of the ideal of modern democracy. If our democracy is strong, there is no need of a separate slogan for secularism. Democracy is based on the recognition of human rights, freedom and equality of all men. The essence of modern democracy is the practice of equality in the society of free human beings who naturally have what has come to be known as human rights. A human right is a right one has by the sheer virtue of being human. But like all such very general notions, when we come to apply them they are bond to have different meanings in situations more characteristic of the particular society in which they are to be applied. It is a paradox of human existence itself that when we apply freedom to social situations, we limit their manifestation. But there is nothing dangerously wrong in this. What it means is that we have to be constantly aware of this feature of human life and in all sincerity to the best of our knowledge without prejudice, interpret the value in such a way so that in that particular situation it realizes the optimum satisfaction. There is no mathematical solution to social problems. Our moral and religious sense of the sacred will always have a role to play. It will stop transgression into prejudice. It will keep us on the side of reason. Strangely, in the times of crises, it is our sense of the sacred that gives us strength. Confusion also prevails because we generally talk of secularism as if it were only to do with politics. But political secularism is just one application of secularism. There is cultural secularism. Cultural secularism is a way of life in which the notion of the sacred has no role to play. There is nothing sacred; there is nothing to be revered. Fortunately, we do not have that situation in India. Though, of course, various social activities, including the way of politics itself, are secular in this sense. For example, it is so in sports. But it is interesting to note that individual sportsmen and women generally begin their venture by invoking their respective gods or goddesses and asking for their blessings. With politician's help from the divine in their elections etc. it is almost universal, except perhaps in the leftist circle. But even there a Sikh politician keeps his turban and the Muslim his typical beard. The opening of various governmental projects are generally done with some worship. It is impossible to eliminate reference to religious faith from Indian life and in this sense a complete secularization of culture is a far cry. Then there is religious secularism too. That means that a man lives his life as an atheist or as a person who has nothing to do with any form of transcendental energy sources. I am deliberately not using the word "supernatural" because in India in spirituality there is no sharp divide between the natural and the supernatural. Religious secularism is a wholly materialistic 'faith', the power of the material is supreme and in this sense it also comes close to a religion. It has a faith in the supreme power, of science and it gives a way of life which has been called "humanism". Needless to say such a faith will be an impoverished religion and will lack many essentially human features, such as a universal morality and a comprehensive ethics including other forms of life and nature.

The point is simply that the terms "secularism" can be applied to any more or less independent and internally cogent form of life, constituting a set of characteristic activities, practices and beliefs. Generally we are talking about politics only. However, in every field the essence of secularism consists in a divorce of religious authority from the practices and the ideals of that field. A complete divorce of this kind is not possible in a society whose way of life is thoroughly inspired by the belief in the sacred power of one divine universe. India is most ideally a religious society of that kind. So it is natural for India to evolve its own version of secularism.

It will be observed now that I have landed myself into a contradiction. It has been my thesis that Indian culture is founded upon Indian spirituality which is embodied predominantly in what has come to be known as Hinduism. And now I see that Indian culture is such in nature that secularism, far from being a competitor, in fact implies secularism. If that is so then according to my thesis a religious society implies a non-religious way of life. And that clearly is a contradiction. Indeed it would be so, if my claim was a general claim about all kinds of religious societies. But it is not. In particular, in thinking about the Indian culture it is certainly not so. There are indeed certain fundamentalist Islamic societies who rightly claim that secularism as the basic form of government is incompatible with Islamic culture. And people naturally have the form of government which they culturally deserve. But there too it is often quoted that the prophet himself made a covenant with the Jews of Madina by which he allowed them to live by their own Jewish laws within a Islamic state. The degree of 'tolerance' implied here also represents a form of secularism, but not a full form of secularism which I see to be implied in the Indian culture. This implication is not despite India being predominantly a Hindu culture but rather because of it. We have seen how Hinduism cannot settle for doctrinal uniformity and consequently to doctrinal fundamentalism. The variety is the very character of Hinduism and unity in diversity is its spiritual message. We have seen how individual freedom of 'faith' is the backbone of the Hindu society. All the same it is highly religious. In such a situation it is only natural for it to have a secular government which accommodates religious sentiments of all the people who constitute the Indian political community. This amounts to having a form of government which gives active support to the wellbeing and flourish of all the religious groups in the country. Let us see how this idea of secularism unfolds itself in practice.

At present two widely different interpretations of "secularism" are in vogue in India. The first one is historically rooted in the history of the West, and its essential thrust is upon the separation of the power of the state from the power of the church. The church represents an organized religious authority which at some point of history happened to take control of the state power as well. Originally it was by the wit of a Roman Monarch who converted to Christianity and declared himself to be the official head of the organized church together with being the head of the state as a monarch. Taken strictly in this narrow sense there is no question of bringing secularism in India, since the religion of the majority Hindus have never been organized along the lines of the churches in the Western world. And no monarch has ever declared himself to be, the head of any religious order as well at the same time. But secularism of this kind has to be taken in its wider implications for a modern democratic state like India. In the modern perspective, where the main job of a democratic assembly is to legislate for a equalitarian governance, secularism means that the laws that are proposed do not invoke the authority of some holy book and their justification is not derived from any scripture or liturgical legislation of any religious order. This much, as we noted earlier, is guaranteed by the secular constitution of the Indian state. As far as I know no political party is even trying to create a Hindu or an Islamic state in the country. What they are frequently tring to do is to launch agitations for securing protection for their preferred religious traditions, places and practices. For example, Muslims are trying to keep Islamic personal law intact even at the cost of equality, to women guaranteed in the constitution. Similarly Hindus, among other things, are trying to rebuild their temples which were destroyed by Muslim invaders and converted into mosques during the past. In some way all Hindus, Muslims and Christians are struggling for making their traditional privileges connected with religious orders, their places of worship and traditions, which under the pressure of globalized economy and modernized culture of consumerism are under great pressure and frequently breaking down. They want in protecting these heritages and traditions that the state should not remain indifferent and should actively support their respective claim as well give financial and other aids as and when necessary. For example, the tradition of going to Hajj to Mecca is kept alive largely by government subsidies. Similarly many places of worship are kept alive because the offerings in these places collected by the mosque or temple act are either not taxed or completely left in the hands of the keepers. As a result some of the places of worship and some of the orders in all religions practiced in India are extremely rich. There is a struggle going on between the holy establishments on the one hand and the state on the other. But in actual practice the state is very charitable and understanding and constantly accommodating the cost of religious sentiments.

This brings us to the second concept of secularism. In Hindi it is called *Sarvadharma Sambhava*. Let us abbreviate it as 'SM'. SM radically differs from the western concept. Far from distancing itself from religion, the state is protecting religion. The politicians frequently demand protective discrimination in favour of this or that religious activity. Politics is often put to the service of religion-related causes. Politicians would ask the public to be voted into power. On the basis of the fact that they are supporting the cause of advancement of a particular religion and betterment of life of the followers of that particular religion. They promise to give more aid to religious schools, sanction governmental aid for building a new place of worship etc. In a democracy it is fair game as long as it does not infringe on the basic rights of citizenship which are common to all the citizens irrespective of their religious affiliations. The same attitude applies to protective discrimination in case of caste, gender etc. In general demands for protective discrimination are considered justified in India and there seems to be no reason why in a democracy particular religious interests should not be politicized. The fear in India against this approach to secularism is that, again in a democracy, the majority community will get away with an unfair share of privileges for the followers of their religion. But surely this will happen in a bad democracy which is not run on equalitarian principles. In a good democracy there are ways of circumventing a misuse of majority power. So the objection against SM does not seem to be an objection against the SM form of secularism. It, however, ought to be an objection against the malpractice of democracy and misapplication of castitarianism. This challenge is always there and it appears in considering discriminative justice in other areas as well. For example, the class of people called "Dalits" or the "exploited" are still kept devoid of socialist justice, of "real equal opportunities for all," by the educated upper classes who belong to upper castes and usually wield power. The Dalits remain backward because their starting point is socially and economically so low that they remain subject to unfair competition. Similarly, in case of secularism Hindus will always get an unfair share of privileges if people and the state are prepared to give it to them simply on the basis of the fact that they are Hindus. Fortunately, this does not happen in India for two reasons. Firstly, the state which in a democracy is found to be run by Hindu majority is safeguarded by the effective working of the judicial system and the respecting of the judicial order by the executive power of the state.

Secondly, respect for all religions is thoroughly embedded in the very structure of the majority Hindu religion. As we noted earlier in the chapter on spirituality, Hindusim itself accommodates a variety of doctrinal differences but united by the principle of "one divine Reality", an inclusive reality of Being called Brahman from which all existence emanates. This has given the ancient belief of *vasudhaeva kutumbkum* meaning literally that "mankind is one family". It is not only a theoretical ideal but a real psychologically operative belief which sets the limits on religious differences to be exploited for political purposes. As all basic political ideals secularism is also a cultural product. And since the Hindu culture is thoroughly informed by universal principles of being together, secularism becomes the natural feature in the practice of politics. In general the SM form of secularism is more appropriate for a thoroughly religious minded society like India. Religion cannot be separated from politics because its ideals determine the ultimate purpose of society and politics is the quest of the most efficient way of realizing that purpose. Religion tells man where his ultimate fulfilment lies so how can politics ignore that part of human existence. It is unfortunate that some religions are very legislative and prescribe conduct in strict form of life. This need not be so. The area of personal freedom in matters of taste and style of living has to be recognized. Both politics and religion need not interfere with that. The purpose of political powers is to create a secure atmosphere for all the people who belong to a nation so that every individual can pursue his interests as creatively as he can. The purpose of political power is not domination of one group by another either within a nation or internationally. This can be most efficiently achieved by the SM form of secularism worldwide. In the contemporary world the concept of a nation cannot be confined to represent a cultural group. Most nations are multicultural. There is no such thing as cultural nationalism. A nation is a political entity and a ereature of history. Nations can easily wither away by a single act of war but cultures do not, though may be shaken and get modified. A religiously inclined nation like India is most suitable to remain a multicultural nation.

A more important point is that the earlier western type of secularism is included in the SM type. The latter is inclusive of all the facet of politics religion relationship. No adherents of SM are demanding a theocratic state in India. Nor are they saying that the majority Hindus should have special rights as citizens over the members of other minority groups. Nor are they demanding that Hindusim should be declared the state religion for the whole of the Indian states and the civil or criminal or general laws should be based in any particular source book of the Hindus. It would be impractical to say the least, since Hindus have various models of ideal governance and they are often not commensurate. They have several source books to serve as the basis for a legal system. Such fears are unnecessary and associated with democracy largely due to political mischief of those who want the Indian state to break up. The SM secularism is mainly demanding two things. One, that on all matter of Hindu religious sentiments they should be taken as seriously as the sentiments of the minority religious groups. Secondly, the majority should also receive proportionately all state help of the kind given to other religious groups. In essence they are simply demanding an equal treatment for all religions and an active support and encouragement by the state to all religions in protecting and strengthening their tradition. All this has to be done with a sensitive eye on the fact that the world is changing in its outlook to keep religions apart from each other and supreme and sovereign in behaviour even when it affects vital state interests. With these qualifications SM type of secularism is certainly indigenous and, therefore, naturally more suitable for this country.

Let us take an example to further classify the issues. At present the hot topic of debate on the question of rights of different religious groups is going on what is known as the "Ayodhya issue". It is common knowledge that the ancient city of Ayodhya is considered the birthplace of the Hindu incarnate God Lord Rama. As such it is considered a holy town, something like Mecca is for the Muslims. It is also common knowledge of history that Muslim invaders from outside India have frequently demolished Hindu temples and on their important sites have instead installed mosques. One such mosque called Babri Masjid, after the 15th century Moghul conquerer Babar, stands on what the Hindus believe to be the site of the birth of Rama and where naturally a temple of Rama stood in the past. (Recently some archaeological excavation has discovered some temple like structure beneath the Babri Masjid. Now what could be the motive behind building a mosque in a city where till then no Muslim population had come up? The obvious answer seems to be that the conquerer was to humiliate the native religion and its people. Given these facts, now in the changed atmosphere of Hindu-Muslim relationship which is by and large friendly, the Hindus are demanding that the government of India should facilitate the recognition of that site by the Hindus who should be allowed to build a temple of Rama. This will restore the dignity of the place, the religion and the Hindu worshippers. This demand is being challenged by the Muslims on the ground that it is violation of India's commitment to secularism. But surely any detached observer can see that the reallocation of the site in question to their morally rightful claimants is not against secularism under SM view of secularism. It is simply a friendly correction of historical chauvinism for the sake of community harmony, and more importantly attending to the justified honour of all religions. It is practicing secularism rather than violating it. SM type of secularism is the saviour of harmonious social relationships between religious groups of different faiths.

We can now sum up our reflection on this matter. Secularism is a very important aspect of culture. The kind of culture of politics it projects shows the level of moral and social achievement the society concerned has achieved. Historically, the word 'secular', in western civilization was used to oppose the church. It came to mean 'belonging to the world and its affairs as distinguished from Christianity". In this negative connotations it was chiefly to signify 'non-ecclesiastical or non-religious". And so secular art, literature, science, technology and even public service will be one which is not concerned with or devoted to the service of religion. In modern times 'secularism' clearly stands for the view that ethics should be founded solely on the considerations of the wellbeing of mankind in the present life excluding all considerations based on the belief in God or afterlife. Similarly, in epistemology secularism aims at establishing an autonomous sphere of knowledge purged of all supernatural presuppositions. In philosophy secularism signifies a revolt against the conception of religion as knowledge. The essence of the matter is that the moral and political authority of religion is to be undermined in all spheres of life and science should be upheld as opposed to faith and revelation. In India this attitude will be wholly rejected until culture itself is exorcised of all religious influence. We see no sign of that so far. Nor is it desirable. We have said that spirituality common to all the religion of Indian origin is the very ground of Indian culture. Moreover, it is difficult to see how religions can ever loose its ultimate significance from human life. Man is not satisfied simply with the immediate and present. He longs to go beyond the senses and even the conceptual mind to establish an intuitive contact with the real being or essence of all existence. The significance for a transcendental ultimate of an eternal truth will always remain for man. Politics is the way man organizes his mundane affairs so that life can be happy and all measures of obstruction in the path of his ultimate fulfilment are removed. How can then politics remain oblivious of its religious needs! It cannot. But given the multi-religious nature of human societies no one religion can dominate over others. Nor can it enslave those who do not believe in God or religion at all. In this context there is a need for secularlism. But it will have to be a democratic secularism which respects human freedom. And this is what has happened in India. We have suggested that the Indian notion of secularism as tolerance of all faiths including atheism is rooted in the Indian cultural soil. It is not an imposition upon people. This does not mean that things cannot radically change in future. But the vision of that future is dim and speculatively unrealistic.

8

THE PHILOSOPHY OF ACTION

The twin doctrines of *Karma* and Rebirth have essentially shaped the Indian philosophy of action. Both the doctrines are wholly accepted by all the religions of Indian origin and naturally influence the unconscious of the people following the religions of other origins since they are almost wholly converts or offsprings of mixed parentage. In any case these other people constitute a small minority and have never stopped sharing the common moral values derived from ancient Indian spirituality.

Popularly stated the doctrine of *Karma* states "as you sow so you reap". The influence of this doctrine is so universal in India that it would be hard to find any individual who does not at some or other time wrote it and some or other time judged his own good and bad destiny in terms of what and how he "sowed". More significantly the doctrine places all human actions in the moral nexus. Every action which a man freely chooses produces a moral as well as a material effect. The influence of this effect is retained as marks in his moral and non-moral character influencing his further choices in future. But these influences while condition his dispositions to choose do not determine his behaviour *absolutely.* At all other times the agent is in principle free to break away from the network of his conditioned me, though of course it will take some inspired insight into his own human condition, or perhaps the grace of gods or a freak of luck etc. Whatever gains the doctrine of rebirth has, are associated with it. But pleasure is repetitive, mechanical and the demand for it becomes a Karmic bondage to the soul. It is, therefore, a negative emotion and has to be avoided as a motive in choosing one's actions. *Krodh* is 'anger', another negative emotion. And *Gita* clearly states that "anger destroys the discriminative power (*buddhi*) in man, and in such a condition a man is easily led to death". One should never act in anger. *Moha* is a complex emotion. Its characteristic feature is *"longing"* for the object of desire. It is an irrational emotion. In *Moha* one tends to cling to the object of desire even if it is self-destructive. It is a pathetic condition akin to madness in which one looses all sense of self-control, rational purpose and integrity. The fourth admonition of *Lobha* is straightforwardly extreme "greed". It is an anti-social, anti-moral and unspiritual negative emotion of the worst kind. It shares many characteristics with *Moha* but it is distinguished from it by its focal concentration on wealth. It is for riches, for wealth in its various forms that one is greedy. But, of course, one can be greedy for power and for recognition as well. It has no limits in its pursuit and can be totally blind to the misery of others. Since the Indian evaluation of virtues and disvirtues work within same teleological framework, having one's life based in these disvirtues are simultaneously considered as spiritually bad for the agent and normally bad for the society. Avoid them and reach out to the highest—the eternal condition of *Brahma-Nirvana* or freedom-in-being.

Acting Without Reward

Does it mean that one doesn't try for self-improvement? The idea has two senses. Let us be clear about it. Take an example, I have a job or perhaps I am a professional musician. I am trying to improve my performance. I practice harder and so on. My aim is to realize the goods internal to music at a higher level. I try to improve my skills. But there is another sense of self-improvement when my effort to improve myself is directed by a motive external to music itself. It may be the motive of getting a higher salary or greater recognition and so on. Then my attempt to improve myself is not directed by the motive of realizing the goods internal to music, i.e. my efforts are not for the sake of music *per se* but for the sake of the psychological 'me', for "becoming", which we have seen is an illusion.

War and Non-violence

"Non-violence" is not a separate determinate phenomenon like 'violence'. In Indian thinking non-violence is a manifestation of the spiritual quality of Love. Socially it is manifest in living together with the moral attitude of "caring and sharing". You cannot *practice* non-violence as a virtue; non-violent living comes about naturally when there is the freedom of Love in the human heart. Love and freedom put together in an individual puts him in the non-violent mode of life. Love which is always 'giving' and 'forgiving' cannot take up violence. It will be contrary to its very essence. Similarly freedom as the natural spontaneity of caring is always creative. Any destructive activity will be contrary to its essence. Being and violence do not go together since the latter brings about non-being. But doesn't sometimes violence become necessary, for example in protecting one's own being? Yes, certainly we have the sacred duty to protect being manifest in all forms of life, and a special responsibility to protect one's own life. Sometimes it may become necessary that in the course of protecting one's own or any innocent person's life one has to resort to force. Let us not call it 'violence' for the latter has moral connotations. Let us call it simply forceful resistance to violence, and only in such cases of *necessity* forceful free resistance is justified. So Ghandhi used to say that forceful resistance as 'violence' is better than cowardice. In a wholly non-violent person violence has no place because he has undergone a total transformation of character imbued with love and the feeling of freedom. So he naturally treats all with impartiality and a tenderness and a sense of justice. This transformed character has eliminated the motives of action connected with egoistic self-assertion and with all personal motives of gain for oneself in prestige, power, wealth etc. His actions will be inspired by motives of love, selfless service to others and love of life in creativity. Such a person is indeed a *mahatma,* that is a 'great soul'.

A society of such selfless individuals will never endorse war for the personal gain of one community against another. The same philosophy of collective motivation of action applies in case of war as the non-violent individual realizes in case of his personal protection. The strong has a sacred duty to protect the innocent and the holy. He has a duty to expel evil from human society. And if in this process for the sake of performing the sacred duty of protecting good it has to go to war it would be justified as an act of forceful resistance or expulsion of evil. But the motive behind war has to be selflessly sacred. The philosophy of war and individual non-violence has been enshrined in the spiritual dialogue between Krishna and Arjuna in the battlefield of *Kurukshetra* and first revealed to mankind in the epic of *Mahabharata*. Ever since its revelation, the Indian culture both in its indivdual and its socially collective forms has been deeply influenced by the ideal of non-violence, right upto the present day. The life of Mahatma Gandhi and his non-violent struggle for Indian independence are examples of non-violence as *"parmodharma"* or the highest order of right action. In its individual aspect it is embodied in the philosophy of non-attachment[1] applied in the day-to-day life, equally by monks and the householder. It is most illuminating to understand this spiritual philosophy as propounded by the Lord himself and most important for getting an insight into the depths of the living Indian culture.

In the *Gita*, Krishna explains to Arjuna how that is or what frame of mind and with what motive, he should act in daily life. He then also gives a justification for acting thus: O Dhananjaya I put aside all attachments, even-minded in success and falure without lamentation and suffering in loss and without an active wish of worldly pleasures.

He first takes note of the bare fact that action is inevitable in life. Even for the minimum subsistence of the body action is a necessary tool. But then going deeper into the matter Krishna unfolds the psychological ontology of action. In a very well known and often quoted verse Krishna explains a hidden complexity of the mechanism of the production of action. We normally consider ourselves as the active doers of action and identify with the will that makes the choices. But Krishna points out that while one has control in the matter of willing a choice one has no control over the actual results of enacted choice. The results that follow are shaped by an enormously powerful network of causes that are independent of the human will. Knowing this truth, Krishna says, act without regarding yourself as the producer of good or bad results and consequently without pride for the former and lamentation for the latter. And, going even further, Krishna says that act in such a manner that inwardly the fruits of the action are not held as your personal motive for acting it.[2] And above all never let inaction hold you back. *This very important passage makes a number of very fine points about the nature of action. But it also lends itself to an interpretation which apparently looks like a self-justifying position. Let us explore the matter further by raising certain objections it might appear to give rise to.*

In the first place we see that Krishna, by advocating that one has no control over the fruits of action is advocating a kind of fatalism. If the results of action flow from hidden causes within a determinative universe then the agent will be so disheartened that he will be never inspired to do anything. Similar dispiritedness is implied in his advocating that the fruits of action should never be made one's personal motive in action. Yet, on the other hand, we are warned of the evil of inaction. Indeed the context is such that Krishna is supposed to be taking Arjuna out of his emotional quagmire and inspiring him to fight, where seeing the nature and extent of the destruction that would be caused by the battle, for whcih he and the army of his opponent cousins are standing in Kurukshetra, he is immensely grieved and refuses to go any further with the war. Arjuna makes his case for inaction that is for dropping out and not fighting thus:

> *O Krishna, seeing our kinsmen and beloved ones standing in opposition for battle my nerves are failing, my mouth is drying up my body is trembling and feelings sinking.....*
> *Moreover I do not see any great virtue in killing our own people. I do not desire a kindom by killing them. What good it is to get that if I have to kill my teachers and elders. I do not want to kill them even if they kill me or take away my kingdom. It will be a sin and how can one be happy by killing one's dear ones! Furthermore, by the destruction of one's kin the whole structure of values will collapse.*

Let us first remove the theoretical hazards before proceeding to see how Krishna makes his case for action and convinces Arjuna to fight the war. The first objection notices fatalism in Krishna's advocacy of war. If the results of action are determined in advance then why act at all? Can one act without desiring a certain result at all?

There is a difference in choosing a course of action for technical reasons as it were, that is because that particular course of action is deemed best for the results wanted and chosing for the sake of personal self-advancement through the realization of those results. Krishna is saying that one should not choose the action for latter reasons. This is for spiritual reasons as well, since spiritually the ultimate goal of life is *Moksha* and choosing a course of acting for person self-advancement produces *Karma* which are binding to the world. Krishna gives his own example that he lives in the world and does all the acts that are necessary for life without desiring the fruits of deeds in a *personal* way. That way actions are not bondage to the world. Let us grasp this philosophy more clearly for it is absolutely central and solves our other theoretical queries as well. There are two types of motives. First a normal person performs an action with the idea of achieving a certain result. In case of technological action one can reasonably expect also a definite result as the casual laws predict. It will be mad to say that one should act without the idea of result and without wanting to affect a definite result. But it is possible that in spite of our best intentions and in spite of our knowledge of the causal laws, the expected results may not follow. In such a case one should not lament and draw oneself in self pity. Krishna is referring to a psychological dimension of gain, which involves the idea of "personal success". Take the example of an ambitious man. He is less concerned with the success of his project *per se.* He is more concerned with the reward in personal psychological dimension where he can feel proud of his achievement and identify with the image of "the successful man". Similarly, for example, a musician can create his music for the love of it but if his eye is on personal success or wealth that he may make, then he will not be inspired to make good music when the wealth is not coming forth. A politician can work for the sake of social justice but if his motive is to get more votes and recognition or power, then his failure will plunge him in self-pity and his work will not yeild the results which he projects in public. At all times, Krishna is saying one's motive should only be "doing the right thing" to bring out the good intrinsic to a given action. At all time one should act either for duty, i.e. to further rightness of the act, or for love of the act but never for the reward of personal benefit of wealth or glory or power. Moreover, there is another higher reason for acting in non-attachment. It is the reward of personal nature that one is attached to. But attachment to such results produces dependence and bondage to *samsara* while the ultimate aim in life should always be *moksha* or the first and last freedom from re-birth and union with God.

So there is no contradiction in Krishna's advice. One must act but rightly, for the sake of goodness and not for the sake of motivations of bondage. In the Indian system the case for right motives is stated negatively, that is, by telling what to avoid and what motives are vices rather than stating a list of positive virtues. This seems right. Virtues keep changing and are open to various interpretation but basic evils are permanent. These are corresponding to the four cardinal desires of *Kama, Krodha, Moha* and *Lobha*. Similarly, there is no contradiction in saying that one should choose consciously and saying that the results are not within one's control.

Further, one very significant point made in the passage under review is that the agent should not consider himself as the actual producer, i.e. the material cause of the results of the action he has chosen. The material production of the results is not in his power. So in this sense the agent doesn't identify himself with the "doer" of action. This seems to give the impression that the agent is exonerated from the moral responsibility for that action. But that is not so. Krishna is making a metaphysically correct point that since the actual results are produced by the complex actual antecedent causes, the person as a self is not the material producer of the results of his action. But he is still responsible for having chosen the action in question. In the material sense, he should not identify himself with the producer of the results and therefore, psychologically he is not to embrace lamentation for the loss and pride and glory for the gainful results. By wrong identification, the mind deceives and the self becomes not only the chooser but also the material producer of the results. Krishna's aim is to enlighten Arjuna in the highest truth of the soul that the agent should not identify himself as the 'doer' of actions. To understand this point one should make a distinction between the consciousness of being the doer of actions and acting without this consciousness. The latter is a creative process in which action is performed without simultaneously assigning it to a psychological self, the 'I' or the 'me'. Acting with the consciousness of being the actor is what is normally going on. It is a process of 'becoming' in the psychological dimension, and is superfluous from the point of view of the actual manifestation of events in the world. In reality the self is not the doer. It has only the illusion of being so for the satisfaction of the ego, and the entanglement of the soul with nature which Krishna states in a religious advice as follows:

> God is seated in the heart of all beings and moves them by the instrument of *Maya* (the illusion of being the doer). Go to his refuge in all your sentiments and you shall receive by his grace, the abode eternal.

In this way Krishna tackles the puzzles of freedom and determination of action and answers the immediate question of fighting or not fighting for Arjuna. His complete answer unfolds itself on three planes—social, moral and spiritual. On the social plain it is a question of his individual interest as a member of the society. And the rightness of the action is to be judged by the criterion of prudence in producing the general good. So he reminds Arjuna that he is by social placement a warrior and it is the duty of a warrior to fight a war if need be so. Fighting is a *Kshatriyas* dharma and by declining that dharma he will be judged as coward and fall in disgrace of his own people as well. It will be imprudent not only to lose the kingdom but more importantly the honour without which living is not worth it. One lives in a society and it is a duty to come up to the societies' expectations in the performance of one's actions. Next, on the moral front war raises the question of justice. Krishna characterizes it as *Dharma yuddha,* i.e. a war of righteousness. An action is justified only if it produces the intrinsic goodness of war. Justice is the intrinsic good of a war. There is no other reason for a war to be fought. And the battle under review is a battle against the most horrible evil. The evil is the entire order of the 'state' which Duryodhana's autocracy has created. No one's human rights are secured. The king is all out for personal gain of wealth and power. All ideas of *dharma* are subjugated to personal pleasure. And what is more painful is that there is no revolt against it. All are blindly following Duryodhana under the vow of loyalty. Krishna invokes an attitude of rebellion. He tells Arjuna that in taking a moral decision one has to stand above the customary traditions. If traditions sustain evil then they have to be abandoned. Krishna's argument introduces a completely new prospect in moral adjudications. Morality of the time was customary and loyalty to the king and one's kinsmen was absolute. The wish as of elders has to be respected at all costs. The other criterion of morality was a fundamentalist interpretation of the scripture. It mostly located action in the personal sphere of observing rituals and rites both inside the home and outside in the community. Krishna rejects both these approaches and introduces the need of personal individual judgement in matter of finding morally right and wrong. This is a turning point in the Indian history of moral practice and Krishna has made a lasting contribution to the culture of ethical independence. Each person has to judge for himself and feel morally responsible for it. Of course one does not judge in a vacuum. All sorts of considerations are relevant and it is a very complex matter. Prudence and considerations of the sacred can't be ignored in making a moral decision. Nor is the individual moral agent an abstract entity. He is at once situated in a moral social and spiritual nexus. And considerations from all these sorts have to be taken into account. That is, an action is a total representation of existence. It manifests at once, an in the material as well as moral and spiritual dimensions. We, as members of a society, cannot dissociate and ignore the spiritual effects of an action from its material effects. Krishna's arguments for Arjuna to act is inclusive in this manner.

To sum up so far, every action has three aspects—material, moral and spirtual. The material results are never within the control of the chooser of the action. So in this sense the ultimate doer, or controller of the results is always God. And consequently, the individual should not lament the non-attainment of those particular results and, for the same reason, he should not take pride in the attainment of the gainful results. One should act with a sense of non-attachment to the results, without making the fruits of action his own motive in acting. On the other hand the moral and spiritual results are contained in the very choosing of a particular course of action. For example, the moral result of an action may be the manifestation of kindness and compassion in the universe and it is attained in being kind itself. And the spiritual effect of it may be the advancement of the cuase of one's liberation. For this reason one should not be attached to inaction and, always choose to act for the sake of the intrinsic goodness of action and never for the extrinsic material results of it.

An important point in this connection is that the Indian philosophy of action works within a teleological framework where the ultimate goal of life is *moksha* or unity with God. Individual purposes to be realized at the empirical level of existence almost add up towards the realization of the God-head or Brahman or *Nirvana,* the first and last freedom from the cycle of rebirths into a final enlightenment. Since human action is spread across a range of rebirths, the results that we are aiming at in the present action should not produce further karmic bondage to the world. This can be achieved if the action in the present realizes the moral and spiritual benefits which are, as we seen, embedded in the very character of the choices one makes. The material results, as we have seen are not within the control of the agent but the moral and spiritual results are. So the individual is always free to advance his cause of liberation. Every act of good intentions and pious behaviour counts. The individual is a traveller on a long journey of seeking the freedom of the soul which is somehow, metaphysically speaking by his own choice of freeplay, is implicated in the order of nature. In the rounds of rebirth he goes on accumulating merits and demerits awaiting a final enlightenment, *Gyan* or the forgotten knowledge of the essence of his soul-nature, which will free him once for all. This much was taught to Arjuna while he was immersed in his sorrow at the thought of the gruesome results to follow from the envisaged battle of *Kurukshetra.* Further, Krishna gave a demonstration of his philosophy of action by giving him a 'vision' of his *viratswarup,* i.e. his "great-body" comprising of his infinite essence as Brahma and all the cosmos emanating from him and returning in him, manifesting through a deterministic universe. The network of the casual laws which determine the universe is an expression of the divine will so in the ultimate analysis freedom and determinism in the universe are two sides of the same coin. The human being constituted by the embodiment of the soul is thus spiritually free and materially determined at the same time. Equipped with this knowledge Arjuna's confidence returns. He is now ready to undertake the battle in non-attachment to its material consequences with the same moral motive of realizing social justice as an expression of acting from non-attachment. There are four cardinal disvirtues recognized in the Hindu scripture and people are dissuaded to make them there own motive or compulsions for action. These are *Kama, Krodh, Moha* and *Lobha.* Respectively they should be understood as follows. *Kama* is the whole spectrum of Desire for sensual pleasures. Pleasure is sharply distinguished from 'joy'. The latter has a spiritual quality to it and spirituality and creativity are natural to it. *Krodh* is the emotion of anger. It is clearly a *reaction* of the self-centred self and therefore, unreasonable. *Moha* is the motive of attachment and the whole philosophy of action we have discussed is based on "non-attachment". Lastly, *lobha* is the straightforward motive of selfishness which, according to this philosophy, has to be put aside at all cost.

NOTE

1. *Gita,* chapter 1, 30-33.

9

TWO CONCEPTS OF LOVE

There seems to be two radically different ways in which mankind has perceived, imagined and relished love. This chapter is an attempt to explore the tension between these two perspectives and if possible to attempt to integrate them. In the first perspective (let me call it 'humanistic love') the word 'love' is being constantly employed in newer and newer contexts, ranging from its most sophisticated uses in poetry to its most reckless and mundane uses in pornographic literature. The humanistic love is what we are most familiar with and can be taken to singnify our ordinary concept of love. In day to day life we are able to make confident judgements about it. We all seem to know the criterion of correct judgement about it, yet we all at times seem to make terrible mistakes in applying it in real life. All the same it is something that we all long for or cannot do without, and when it comes upon us we helplessly fall pray to it. The Greak philosopher Empedocles has said that it is some universal force that help the world together and pervaded all living beings; while in common parlance it is said that love is what makes the world go round. Love is what we seek from other human beings, especially the opposite sex. It signifies a very special kind of relationship between those who claim to love each other. It dose not seem to have an opposite or parallel. Hate is not the opposite of love, since clearly when you stop hating a person you don't *ipso facto* start loving her. It is this humanistic sense of love in which one is said to 'fall in love' sometimes at first sight, and also in this sense one is said to fall out of love at appropriate time or else, unfortunately, one may have to suffer it out when one is no longer himself receiving it from the other. But the net of love can be cast very wide. The special relationship that it involves can be held not only with a person of the opposite sex but with any other person, and with people where sex is not involved at all. Obviously one uses the word to refer to one's ralationship with one's mother or sister or daughter or someone who has the status of being 'just a friend'. This shows quite obviously that sex is not essential to the relationship of love : it is just one of the many different kinds of acts one may engage in under that title.

From the above brief reflection on the general character of love, we can see that two of its features seem to stand out as important. One, that it is always directed upon a particular object, paradigmatically a human person. And only in a secondary sense it may be seen to apply to other things or animals etc. And secondly, that humanistic love seems to demand reciprocity. Even in case of loving an inanimate object we expect it to give us a feeling of security perhaps, or some form of pleasure. In its most mundane usage to say 'I love coca cola' is to imply that one derives satisfaction in consuming it, and to say 'I love tennis ' is to imply that one gets a feeling of thrill in playing it or watching it played. The other feature of directedness is not too surprising as, per Brentano's thesis, it is a typical feature of all consciousness, " In presentation something is presented, in judgement something is affirmed or denied, in love loved, in hate hated, in desire desired, and so on."[1] The key to the understanding of humanistic love lies, I think, in understanding these two features in terms of their contents. For this reason it would be better to explore these features through more concrete consideration of the relation of "being in love" with another person.

Love is not the name of a single type of act like 'running', for example. It is not something that we can be doing or performing over a period of time. We cannot choose to start loving for sex, for example, the next ten minutes from now. We cannot switch on and switch off loving at will. When you say 'I made love with her', you know what it means. Pleasure is surely not the main outcome of love. The outcome of love is supposed to be 'happiness', which is a holistic quality of life, something more sublime and more difficult to define, than pleasure, which is a mere sensation. Again 'love' is not the name of a particular sensation or feeling or even a particular emotion; all of which float in and float out of consciousness in marked spaces of time. When one is in love with a person, his eyes certainly glow up when he sees her, and certain feelings and emotions certainly float in as appropriate, but being in love *per se* dose not signify a single type of feeling or emotion. One is not hooked on to a particular emotion day and night, as it were, as long as one is in love with a particular person. Nor is it a state of mind characterized by thought-awareness. When one is in love one need not be thinking of the person one loves all the time. Indeed when the lover is engaged in his creative pursuits or absorbed in whatever else he loves doing, he is not at all aware of the person he loves. This does not mean that during those intervals he had stopped loving the person in question. It seems then that though it is far from being an emotional state or thought-awareness, it has some active psychologically significant component. Being in love is not a wholly passive state. One cannot remain completely neutral to or with respect to a person and yet claim to be in love with that person. If I an in love with a woman surely I am suitably disposed to get into certain mental and physical states on certain suitable occasions in relation to her, and often actually do that without overtly exhibiting them. I must have loving and caring thoughts about her. I must desire to spend time in her company, and to share other activities of life with her. I must have certain appropriate feelings and emotions in relation to her and so on. If I do not ever manifest any of these mental states in relation to her, then surely I couldn't still go on to claiming that I nevertheless loved her. And further the test of these mental states lie in their expression. In general the proof of the pudding is in the eating. I think one would generally agree with these observations. Love must have its realization in actual mental and physical life. But now we must work out their further implications. It seems to me, firstly, that humanistic love is necessarily embodied in specific forms of human relationship. It is inter-personal. One loves individual persons and relates to them in mental and physical postures which are appropriate to their natural and social status. This is the primary case of humanistic love, and only in a secondary, derivative sense one talks of one's love of specific arts and objects of the natural or the manufactured world. We can safely conclude then that in so far as love is an emotion it is a very special kind of emotion, a complex emotion, unlike other familiar emotions such as anger, fear or depression. One does not get into swings of love and get out of it at particular moments. 'Out of sight and out of love' is not the case with lovers. Love creeps over you rather quietly. One may not even often realize that one was in that way to so and so. And the moment of realization is not the moment of falling in love . The expression "falling in love", in its temporal accretions is simply a metaphor, and so is the expression "love at first sight ". Let us now explore the concept further by raising the question of the necessary and sufficient conditions for someone to be said to be in love with another person. And for that let us first lay down intuitively, what other mental states are involved in the extraordinary state of being in love with a person.

We have agreed that love though itself is not the name of a simple emotion, the presence of certain appropriate emotions seem to be strong indications of the presence of love. Apart from these relevant emotions, love seems to involve a complex set of intentions, attitudes and desires, all of which, I will argue are necessary though not sufficient for the state of love. These mental states are intentional in the sense that they are necessarily directed towards their objects. Thus a person in love with X is likely to have the intentions involving goodwill towards X. He will frequently intend or want to do things which he believes are good for the loved one. Are these intentions necessary to being in love? It seems very difficult to deny that they are so. But these intentions may be unconscious and the lover may not know that he has them. That is they are not necessary in the sense of being self-consciously occurrent states of mind. The lover will no doubt act with great goodwill towards X, but he may not record any occurrent loving-intentions in advance of their execution. The lover may simply act quite spontaneously towards X, in a manner which will be subsequently described as an exercise in the manifestation of a loving intention. The manifestation of love in spontaneous behaviour embodying goodwill is obviously not a sufficient indication of the presence of loving intention, since the behaviour in question may be sponsored by something higher and more inclusive such as compassion, or perhaps the Kantian sense of Duty.

Next, how shall we read the 'attitudes' involved in love? It will be generally agreed, I think, that the lovers attitude towards X must be that of caring, trust and sincerity. These attitudes are necessary. But attitudes are not occurrent states of mind. They signify dispositions which will manifest quite spontaneously as and when relevant conditions obtain, and the agent may be unaware of the fact that he has those dispositions. Again these attitudes do not seem to be sufficient for establishing the claim of being in love with X. These attitudes are not exclusively linked to 'love', and can easily be directed upon persons whom one does not love as such. These attitudes are more indicative of the type of person one is rather than of what relationship one has with some other person.

Next, I have suggested that love necessarily involves certain mental states of the nature of desire. In fact intending presupposes some kind of wanting or desiring to be thus and so in relation to a particular person. But in case of love there seem to be necessarily involved some self-fulfilling or self-gratifying desires. Doesn't the lover want, to put it euphemistically, the prolonged company of the loved one? Doesn't the lover also want a certain kind of attention and behavioural response from the loved one? And to put it the whole hog, doesn't the lover want nothing short of being loved himself by the loved one? I think the answar to these musings are in the positive. Ideally, that is, the lover does desire to be loved himself. This relation of the desire for reciprocity seems to be at the heart of the humanistic love. And there is clearly a basis for it. A natural attraction to the other seems to be the basis of desire for reciprocity. This feeling of attraction has both biological and psychological ingredients. Sexual attraction is a clear example of the biological attraction. While what we call the 'charm' of a person is a clear indication of the psychological attraction. The cause of the psychological attraction is supposed to be hidden in the depths of our childhood conditioning. All in all the role that the natural attraction to the other plays in fomenting love is most important. For it enables us to launch our loving intentions, desires and attitudes in real relationships and to experience the feelings and emotions that go into the flowering of love in that relationship. Feelings of attraction, as in case of pleasure, necessarily promote desire to get indulgent with them and to seek fulfilment in real relationship, just as, conversely, a feeling of pain naturally promotes desire to get rid of it. In real life, without such a basis, it is difficult to see, given that love is not a mere intellectual achievement, how could a person ever initiate the relevant desires, intenions and attitudes.

We are now in a position to sum up the preceding reflections on the subject. I have suggested that humanistic love signifies a complex state of mind. It involves natural states of attraction and active feelings of affection and attachment pouring on to the loved one. It involves intentions imbued with goodwill and pro-attitudes of protective engagement and discrimination towards the loved one. It can evoke a variety of emotions in relation to the loved one, depending upon her condition and the nature of her situation in life. At the same time love has its own demands, desires and expectations from the loved one. At times it can turn very demanding and possessive. And, if frustrated, it can threaten to destroy the beauty of the relationship altogether. It can feel terribly insecure and approach the loved one with suspicion, caution and manipulation. At other times, however, it may appear powerfully self-confident, generous, insouciant, almost immortal, and shinning with the beauty of the purity of heart. All in all it stands for a dynamic relationship between two people, demanding mutuality in fulfilment, recognition and compassion. Indeed, because of this subjectivity, it seems, that only if you are yourself in love that you can truely appreciate, or even recognize, the other's love for you. Yet, we also come across cases, especially in the oriental culture, in which love is almost wholly passive, representing a surrendered state of mind, waiting to obey any call from the loved one. Such a lover seems to have no particular desire or intention of its own, nor is it engaged actively in feeling any emotions or protecting some specific sentiment.

In all cases, however, the peculiar mixture of the various ingredients of love produce their own variety of cocktails. Thus we come to speak of the various qualifications of love its intensity, sincerity, depth, passion and charisma. In actual life the course of love is most unpredictable, and its manifold manifestations shine and glitter in a variety of sheens. It is not always possible to say which set of the combination of the various elements of love does actually constitute love proper or true love. Helplessly, one can only speak negatively, that if none of the required ingredients are present, then surely a claim to be in love could be quite empty.

The mysterious nature of love is quite obvious from the fact that both in its fulfilment and in its frustration, people tend to behave in hideous and variously supererogative ways. In frustration the range varies from committing suicide to taking the life of the loved one itself. In the fulfilment of love we know that the lover can move mountains; if he has to make incredible sacrifices; while at the other end of the spectrum, he can be extremely mean and self-centred. There seem to be no standard ways of realizing love, nor standard ways of approaching the loved one. Faced with such a variety of presentation and experience of love, it is almost impossible to lay down the logically necessary and sufficient criteria for it. Yet we all seem to know the difference between a real or true love and a fake or insincere one. Perhaps the way we make this assessment lies in our subjective assessment of how far love should allow the lover to be self-seeking in relation to the beloved. We have noted that the desire for reciprocity is at the heart of the humanistic love. In fact desire evoked by love is always, at least covertly, self-dedicated. The lover may try to possess her completely. But as Sartre has ingeniously pointed out that even a success in possessing is not satisfactory. This is so because the beloved is to be possessed as a free person, and not a slave. And there is an inherent contradiction in the idea of possessing someone else's freedom completely. To make her *want* you is another stratagem. But if that is encouraged by satisfying her own lust and fancies, then that too is not satisfactory. You do not want her to want you if it is not evoked by her own love for you. As we have seen, what you want is that she desires you for her own love's sake, that is, from the purity of her love, as it were. But I have suggested that there is no such thing as 'pure' love, if that is meant to signify a state of being in love without the desire for reciprocity. So one has to make a compromise somewhere. But the terms of the compromise is the problem; it involves a subjective assessment of where to draw the line. Our idea of howmuch self-interest counts as selfishness varies a lot. And howmuch of my self-love is going to be allowed to pass as my love-need depends upon the subjective perdispositions of the other. So the lime between real and insincere love is not open to objective determination.

These reflections reveal an important feature of love. The lover wants to be loved by the other and at the same time, ideally at least, wants the other to be completely un-self-seeking. And, in the human situation, this seems ot be an impossible state of affairs. Indeed it is paradoxical, for to want to be loved and not want to be treated in some or other way as an 'object' for the lover's own fulfilment is contradictory. And the same goes for the lover. That is, to want to love another and pretend to be wholly un-self-seeking is an impossible human situation.

This is the place where the talk of spiritual love gets a foothold in the discourse. The spiritual love stands in complete contrast with the humanistic love. First of all the spiritual love is not directed upon a person, not even a divine being such as the personal God. In my taxonomy, the love of God invoked in theistic religions falls under the humanistic love, for, clearly, the relation of reciprocity is considerd most significant in them. The believer loves God to seek His care and protection *on account of* God's love for all his children. And the contradiction I have noted in this context, is also involved in God's attitude towards his children. For, God is supposed to require their 'pure love' from them—love, that is, devoid of all motives of self-interest. The spiritual love I am thinking of is not to be found in theistic religion, but in the poems and the philosophies of mysticism. For example, the following poem by Kabir sets the stage for its further exploration :

When it is I
then Thou is not
When Thou reveals in me
the I dissolves;

The lane of love
is too narrow
for both you and I
to promenade.

In this poem Kabir seems to envisage a state of mind in which the lover is completely absorbed in the consciousness of some higher spiritual reality, so much so that not only his self-love but his self-consciousness altogether is abolished by that immensity. Such a state of mind is quite unselectively giving and caring without any motive of self-gain whatsoever. It seems to resolve into a kind of universality which has no focus or object of love, and which is free from all forms of attachment to individual persons. But before I dwell upon this insight on this subject we must consider the following complexity.

It may be suggested that though the humanistic love is generally demanding reciprocity, it can also be at times wholly self-sacrificing and self-abandoning. So it is important to distinguish this brand of selflessness from the one that is required by the spiritual love. In order to reveal this difference, therefore, we need to probe into the psychology of self-sacrifice. In particular we need to determine if it is not the case that the humanistic self-sacrifice is always, at least covertly, self-motivated. On the face of it there seem to be two types of motives which lurk behind the cases of self-sacrifice. These are: the feeling of psychological security, the gathering of self-esteem and protection of the self-image.

There is no dubt that the thought of loosing one's beloved or losing her love for you is most frightening. Now, it seems to be the case that deepdown there it is this fear that prompts one to contemplate making all kinds of sacrifices. The deeper the sense of insecurity in a person, the stronger his bonds of attachment will be. And the thought of the breaking up of that bond will be most disturbing. The sense of insecurity generated by that thought can easily drive one into making extraordinary sacrifices, if they are seen to protect the bond. Without that bond life would appear to be meaningless, and the lover would experience a kind of death of the self, which again is most intolerable. So, clearly, the role that self-sacrifice is playing here is to strengthen the bond, and secure the feeling of the continuity of the self. Self-sacrifice in this case then, is not at all a case of self-abondonement. Similarly, people want to fall in love for self-esteem, just as much as they want to be loved themselves. They want to fall in love because they hold the idea that life without having fallen in love, at least once in life, is not adventurous enough to feel favourable in ones own eyes. They think favourably of themselves if they have proved it to themselves. And to do that they have to make gestures of self-sacrifice. They need to be recognized as thus and so by the beloved as well as by the world. This game they play with themselves can land them into much display of sacrifices they are capable of making, often involving real losses in material security. Thus once again the sacrifices they make are self-reflexive, as they have an eye to their own well-being. Finally, the motive of self-image in making sacrifices enters in love-making in two ways. On the one hand the idea that one is a hero of sacrifice may genuinely be an ingredient into one's exiting self-image. That is, one may be beliveing oneself to be a genuine self-sacrificing person anyway. It is then only a welcome step if one has to do that for the sake of one's own love. Moreover one must protect one's self-image at any cost. The self-image is one's ideal self-identity. And if protecting it calls for much self-sacrifice, so be it. In another way one may be consciously projecting a self-image of that kind.The sacrifices made in that regard are clearly made to serve the further end for which the projection is designed. Again the self-sacrifices curl upon the self which initiates them.

These conclusions should not surprise us. For, as we have already seen, the attraction to the beloved, which is the natural basis of the humanistic love, always carries some desire favouring the self-satisfaction of the lover. Thus, a motiveless sacrifice is not the natural compliment to the basis of love. Since desire is always covertly self-dedicated, self-sacrifice must always have some personal motive. For the human self, giving must always be a self-seeking. In the human situation, in the normal course, things cannot be otherwise. However, I am not suggesting, that for this reason, sacrifices in love become less genuine and loose their value. As I have already suggested, that the line between the genuine and false love has to be drawn elsewhere. All the same it presents a point of contrast with the spiritual love. If we think of sacrifice as a manifestation of virtue, as we do, then it should not be guided by the motive of self-love in any form. A virtuous act is one which is performed for realizing the good 'internal' to the act. This would not be possible if sacrifices are made under pressure from the conditioned background of insecurity, self-esteem, or the need to protect one's self-imge. Only in freedom form these there can be the genuine virtue of self-abandonement.

In a similar vein, Sartre has maintained that love is an impossible state of affairs. For, firstly, in love each person tries to 'possess' the other, and then, each person tries to free himself from the possessive "look of the other". If one side surrenders and chooses to be possessed, then that would take away the feeling of conquest of the other, and then it is hardly worth it, for then, the possessed is a mere 'object' and not a person. This exposes a deep fallacy in the idea of the humanistic love. In love one wants to possess the other as well as keep him as an independent self. It considers that object of desire in an impersonal way as instrumental to living one's life as a human being. One desires food for example, when one is hungry. And one desires nutritious and even tastier food because one recognizes the overall importance of emotional balance for good health. But, if one is lustful or crazy or craving for a particular kind of food, then the element of "becoming" comes in. Then there is attachment with the object of desire. Attachment involves psychological dependence. One cannot do without the object of desire, in the sense of deriving personal existence in its satisfaction. Without it one's fear being reduced to a "no-thing". The ideal of pure love is the jewel of Indian culture. Pure love is not attachment. There is no desire to possess or to belong to the person one loves. It involves a wholly selfless state of consciousness with respect to the object one loves. Pure love is freedom. It has no motive of personal gain in relationship. It is always sharing and caring. Such affectionate and compassionate acceptance of the other can arise only from the background of total selflessness, which does not see the other as an object of usefulness or manipulation. In Indian culture this ideal is hidden in every heart, even though, life being what it is, one often fails to embrace it. Pure love of God is the mark of a saint or a holy man, which lifts him above the divisions of faith into the universal kingdom of mankind. In India *bhakti*-poetry and *bhakti-sangeet* (music) dedicated to the divine is a most popular strand of culture. In person to person relationship pure love enters even popular movies and all other performative arts. Among the village folk, eulogies of famous love stories is a popular cultural act.

It is not easy to get at the understanding of what love is directly. So one has to approach it through its negations, by feeling one's way with phenomena close to love which we normally tend to identify with it. One such phenomenon is pleasure, especially some form of sexual pleasure. When we are deriving sexual pleasure from the other, we think that we are loving the other. But sexual pleasure is based in sensation which, by its nature, demands continuity. Any violation of the continuity is met with frustration and often violence to the other. Such a situation can hardly be characterised as love. Moreover the pleasure is stored in memory and further demands for it are occasioned by internal stimuli. Such demands create dependence upon the object of desire which we have seen is not love. Dependence is bondage to the past, while love is freedom in moment to moment awareness of the new. Clinging to the past is an expression of insecurity. In love there is a sense of completeness. So there is no comparison with the past and consequently no sense of insecurity. It does not demand reciprocity. This ideal of pure love is perhaps the greatest achievement of the Indian culture.

10

POSTSCRIPT

In todays world, the consolidated effect of modernity, the picture of man as the rational autonomous individual endowed with free-will is complete. The individual is 'individualistic': self-interested, egoistic, clamouring for more and more power, wealth and social status. He has stopped thinking about life considered *as a whole.* There is no overall spiritual meaning to life. His life is divided between purposes which are contingently thrust upon him by his environment, requiring fulfilment with a speed and efficiency which occlude any evaluation of their meaning for life as a whole. Indeed he finds it difficulty to apprehend "life as a whole", to consider it as a unity, except chronologically. As MacIntyre in his most perceptive discussion of the contemporary scene observes: "... Modernity partition's each human life into a variety of segments, each with its own norms and modes of behaviour. So work is divided from leisure, private life from public life, the corporate from the personal. So both childhood and old age have been wrenched away from the rest of human life and made over into distinct realms. And all these separations have been achieved so that it is the distinctness of each and not the unity of the life of the individual who passes through those parts in terms of which we are taught to think and to feel."[1] Moreover the very character of "the social" has changed so much, as many post-modern thinkers have emphasized, that the individual need not even bother about the 'unity of life' and its overall inclusive end to provide a teleological framework for his endeavours. 'The social' no longer demands conduct in which human relationships are informed by *virtues.* Indeed most social institutions of the past which provided for the cultivation of virtues and the qualities of character in the individual have either totally disappeared or have been rendered underdetermined by the vast changes in the character of relationships sought by the individuals. This is the age of shifting relations of interdependencies, where even the most basic forms of human bonds—pair relations, sexuality, family, kinship and friendship for example—have become institutionally undetermined. The individual is faced with the stark reality of a communitarian alienation and competitive insecurity. The notion of rational autonomous subject has been taken to its rediculous limits—freedom into anarchy, individualism into self-centred egoism, rejection of the substantial self into total fragmentation. The blemishes that have warped our ethical consciousness and disfigured our conscience are many, but perhaps, the most serious one emerges ironically, though unselfconsciously, from what must be considered as the virtue of modernity. Modernity which brought *freedom* from the unthinking callous 'authority' of various non-secular traditions went too far and liberated the hidden greed lying curled up in the human heart.

But surely, in the culture of greed-statisfaction there is no hope for *peace*—peace, as a cultural realization must manifest itself first in social spaces of interpersonal attitudes, intentions and relationship.

The extent of degeneration in the values of interpersonal relationship is obvious when we realize that in todays world we have come to need a *justification* for treating others equally and impartially—the rational precept which could provide the underpinnings for law. And philosophers have discussed the question "Why should I be moral?" And if we need to discriminate 'protectively', in favour of those who are severely marginalized, we need a "veil of ignorance" about their real human status so that we can be convinced in our hearts that we are not being unfair to ourselves in going out of way to help the needy. In this extraordinary situation we find that the ethics of compassion, love and caring has suddenly ceased to be relevant. There may be no basic 'given' (eternal) structure of human relations but, under the surface of sophistication, it certainly, seems to have *become* what Hegel's famous image of "master-slave" anticipated. Even the most ardent believer in human freedom, Sartre, succumbed to its temptations. "While I attempt to free myself from the hold of the Other, the Other is trying to free himself from mine; while I seek to enslave the Other, the Other seeks to enslave me. We are by no means dealing with unilateral relations with an object-in-itself, but with reciprocal and moving relations......within the perspective of *conflict.* Conflict is the original meaning of being-for-others".[2] We need not accept this verdict upon the nature of interpersonal attitude, as a description of the fundamental, ontological, structure of human relationship, but as a correct representation of what has *become* of it, it is surely undeniable. We face each other with the motive to prevail over the other, in a moving situation of perpetual conflict.

The individual is oriented towards ends which are discrete, unrelated, making for no coherent ethos or even style of life. But what is most frightening is the ethical and aesthetic dislocation of sensibility. The aesthetic consciousness is 'ingrown', has lost communion with nature and the life of the universe as a whole. It is churning out stuff in the name of self-expression, as though 'self-expression' was the highest form of a characteristically human achievement. It has forgotten to take note of what has *become* of the human self (a social product, conditioned in its virtues and vices) which has grown on the stage of 'conflict' and which has accumulated all the filth of the consumerist modernity. There is a point where the line between life and death is too thin, just as the line between art and vulgarity, but the line all the same there is. That we fail to recognize it only shows that we have forgotten what it means to be an Artist of life.

The world of human relationships has lost its intrinsic worth. The world is 'my' world in which everything is organized instrumentally for the satisfaction of some undefined, intangible need of personal 'security' and personal individual fulfilment. The fragmented life of this divided individual is glowing with the feeling of the fear of 'being left out' of the race—an insecurity whose origin and character he is blissfully totally ignorant of. Man is lost in the wilderness of civilization of his own cultivation.

The loss of the ethical perspective upon life both in thought and in social action is evident enough. For the former, the modernity having admirably freed the moral agent from the stifling hold of the esoteric authority of 'revelation' and the blind precepts of superstition, landed him into the hands of another, equally esoteric authority of "rational intuition". God may have died (per Nitzsche) but man could not have killed him. Perhaps he committed suicide in utter disillusionment and frustration over his pride creation. And again having unhooked the understanding of the moral agent from the mysteries of 'foundationalism' and 'essentialism', modernity has thrown him into the hands of the unmerciful loneliness and uncertainty of his *subjectivity*. The modern moral agent, devoid of any inner spiritual strength, dependent upon the externals, and lacking reference to the 'ultimate worth' of his activities, is constantly afraid of loosing, or being too late to collect, the 'visible' and immediately affective pleasures of life. He is left with no choice but to continue to struggle in the pursuit of his own personal achievements with a sustained drive, greed and competitiveness so characteristic of the contemporary engagement with life. And such choice, in turn, has landed us into deeper crises. The, by now, familiar environmental crisis is nothing but an outer aspect of an inner crises of meaninglessness in the ethical consciousness.

As for the loss of the ethical perspective in social action, the degenerate state of culture and politics relationship is ample evidence. The cultural politics has turned into the 'politics of culture'. Moreover, the fragmentation and short sightedness of political enterprises world over exposes the ethically ambivalent, inner state of mankind.

On the one hand being egoistic, and realizing that everyone is trying to get *there* (God knows where) first and possess as much as he can, he just submits, in a *quasi* Hobbesian manner, to the rule of law, apparently based on the moral idea of equality. On the other hand, being impelled by the desire to dominate over others, (as we saw in the primary structure of human face-to-face) he must try to seek power in all forms and ways accessible to him. He must then (unconsicously perhaps) introduce loopholes in the systems of the society, in particular of laws, and hope to retian control over them through a system which has all the pretentions of 'equality' but inherently open to subversion by the cleverer and stronger. He thus submits to the rule of law (allows the law to take its own course) only to ensure a smooth transition to his desired inequality. His purposes are best served in the installation (perhaps) of the modern liberal democracy.

The social ideal of justice and democracy which the Western Enlightenment admirably struggled to realize; is inherently aporetic—based upon a deep contradiction in the modern consciousness. We are contend to believe that though the liberal democracy is not perfect, it is the best that can be realized. Or those who are not so pessimistic are content with the thought that human rationality would one day find a resolution. But even if a rational resolution could be found it will be limited and short lived,we cannot install the gains of reason into new institutions. The old institutions are fast loosing their grip on reality, if not already dead or rendered ineffective. And the new would need infinite flexibility and versatility to cope with the infinite disorder in the fragmented but fast reshaping river of *all* consciousness. Shattered beings can best represent reality in bits and pieces.[3] The resolution of the conflict cannot come from the readymade 'objective' social morality, from determinate moral rules to be followed or virtues to be cultivated, or from the calculations of the greatest good of the greatest number. For, as Zygmint Bauman[4] has observed, "... morality is endemically and irredeemably non-rational—in the sense of not being calculable, hence not being presentable as following impersonal rules, hence not being describable as following rules that are in principle universalizable. The moral call is thoroughly personal; it appeals to my responsibility, and the urge to care thus elicited cannot be allayed or placated by the awareness that others do it for me, or that I have already done my share by following to the letter what others used to do ... Being moral means abandoned to my freedom."

Today we are faced with making a resolute choice between getting swallowed up by a culture thrust upon as by the dictates of a technocratic capitalism, and working towards creating a culture sensitive to the spiritual dimensions of human existence which respects nature and life in all things. This choice cannot be made by the 'collective'; it is not a politico-economic choice. It can be made only by a 'true' individual, who, unfortunately, somehow lost his way in the new industrial metropolices.

The contemporary critics tend to overidentify the ills of capitalist modernization, which encouraged monopolization and misuse of power, which distorted knowledge to suit manipulative techniques for economic subordination, with the rather honest and noble intentions of intellectual modernization to create a rational and scientific approach to knowledge and social progress, and consequently, wrongly identify the aggressive individualism encouraged by the former with an essentially ethical individualism of the latter. The intellectual modernity rejected the grounding of practical reason in blind 'authorities' of occult subjectivity both in matters of morals and in objective truth. And by and large (notwithstanding the claims of 'rational intuition') placed a premium on the honest, dispassionate and unprejudiced judgement of the individual, *in the final analysis.* But the spirit of their enterprise left all judgements open to revision, though no doubt always aiming at objective finality. In this attempt they, perhaps unappreciatively, invoked the authority of the 'ethical' in final adjudications of all truth claims. The individual had to feel responsible for his truths and social commitments, and had to arrive at them through honest impartial considerations. Such individualism is not dictatorial or idiosyncratic. It is another matter that this healthy individualism lost its battle for humanizing culture against ruthless capitalism, and grew into a "fat and selfish" egoism.

The upshot of this brief reflection on the odds and evens of some contemporary myths and insights is to invite us to give the devil its due, to face ourselves and realize that any programme of social action for cultural regeneration stipulated by the seminarists, curls up upon the participants considered as individuals. It is the individual human being in whom alone there lies, first and foremost, the creative energy needed for cultural transformation. He must somehow realize that *he* is responsible for the way the world is today—violent, uncaring, unsharing and unloving—not he alone nor he collectively, but he individually. And this means that social action must begin from action upon himself—the action of making ourselves integrated beings, 'whole', and true individuals. This would require the discipline of self-knowing, of understanding oneself as a *total process.*

To transform the acquisitive culture of conflict and aggression into a culture of peace of care, man must return to himself, perceive the hidden motivational springs of his action and in knowing himself thus and so, discover the sacredness of life, of nature and the wholeness of his interrelatedness with it. As it is, the culture we have created, which in turn has conditioned us, is the result of our constant endeavour to succeed and dominate to acquire personal power in some form or the other, as separate beings. It is a sad story of human misery and suffering and endless conflict. Each one of us is composed of those cultural universals. One has to realize, not only intellectually, but experientially in the structures of one's consciousness, perceive the truth that "we are the world and the world is us". "The world is in each of us; to feel that, to be really committed to it and to nothing else, brings about a feeling of great responsibility and an action that must not be fragmentary, but whole."[5] The culture for peace is the way of life of the individuals who have put themselves on the road to total freedom—freedom from the conditioned dictates of the accusitive culture. Such individuals do not succumb to pressures for the blind run for what glitters like gold but alas! melts away like wax. The promised land of happiness through single minded devotion to material (industrial) growth is a mirage whose true nature one fails to see in the culture which has given us the unquenchable thurst for 'more'. We must assume responsibility for regenerating the culture for peace through re-making ourselves into integrated wholes, beings that are at peace with themselves, then the spiritual quality of the feeling of unseparateness of the 'me' would enable us, naturally and quite spontaneously, to relate to others in love, freedom and understanding. Then there will be a culture which will achieve great heights of Truth, Goodness and Beauty, but without any sense of personal glory, power, achievement and superiority over others. Such a culture will be an act of creativity and not of a competitive struggle.

NOTES

1. Alasdair MacIntyre, *After Virue,* Duckworth, 1981, p. 190.
2. J.J. Krishnamurti, *Unconditionally free,* KFI, 1995, p. 34.
3. To echo Rainer Maria Rilke: "Shattered beings are best represented by bits and pieces".
4. *Postmodern Ethics,* Blackwell, U.K., 1993, p. 60.
5. J.P. Sartre, *Being and Nothingness,* New York, 1956, p. 474.

INDEX